THE ZEN [

Ryōkan

(Frontispiece) *Ryōkan's birthplace.*

List of errata

1. p.18   4 line from the bottom

    1970 $\longrightarrow$ 1790

2. the back cover   3 line from the top

    1757 $\longrightarrow$ 1758

3. the back cover   6 line from the top

    seventeen $\longrightarrow$ eighteen

4. the back cover   3 line from the bottom

    Hikosaku Yanagashima

    $\longrightarrow$ Hikosaku Yanagishima

5. p.121   the top of the page

    かたみとて　なにかのこさむ　春は花

    山ほととぎす　秋はもみぢ葉　（良寛）

THE ZEN FOOL

Ryōkan

Misao Kodama
&
Hikosaku Yanagishima

CHARLES E. TUTTLE COMPANY
Rutland, Vermont & Tokyo, Japan

I heartily thank my bosom friend, Mr. John M. Rasche, who has always helped and encouraged me, sharing Ryōkan's spirit.

Published by Charles E. Tuttle Publishing,
an imprint of Periplus Editions (HK) Ltd.

©1999 by Charles E. Tuttle Publishing Co., Inc.

LCC Card No. 98-89825
ISBN 0-8048-2128-3

First edition, 1999

Printed in Singapore

Distributed by:

USA
Charles E. Tuttle Company, Inc.
Airport Industrial Park
RR1 Box 231-5
North Clarendon, VT 05759
Tel: (802) 773-8930
Fax: (802) 773-6993

Japan
Tuttle Shokai Ltd.
1-21-13 Seki
Tama-ku, Kawasaki-shi
Kanagawa-ken 214-0022, Japan
Tel: (81) (44) 833-0225
Fax: (81) (44) 822-0413

Southeast Asia
Berkeley Books Pte Ltd.
5 Little Road #08-01
Singapore 536983
Tel: (65) 280 3320
Fax: (65) 280 6290

Tokyo Editorial Office:
2-6, Suido 1-chome,
Bunkyo-ku, Tokyo 112-0005, Japan

Boston Editorial Office:
153 Milk Street, 5th Floor
Boston, MA 02109, USA

Singapore Editorial Office:
5 Little Road #08-01
Singapore 536983

Contents

PHOTOGRAPHS
(by Hirotake Motojima)

Gogo An II.

Introduction

In the following pages, we will present to you a Buddhist monk. We believe that through understanding what he represents, you will come in direct touch with the quintessence of the Japanese mind. Indeed, he may be seen as a spiritual model for us all. We hope that you will also feel this to be true after reading these pages.

It is more than one hundred and fifty years since he breathed his last and now his name is quite familiar with many people in Japan. Today he has come to be looked upon as a man of such mettle and character that everybody cannot but feel encouraged and smile even at the very mention of his name, Ryōkan.

It is said that once a lean monk came up Mt. Kugami[1] and nestled down, like a bird gone astray, in a small hut[2] that had been left alone halfway up the mountain nearly two hundred years ago. It was only a shabby hut; but to him who had lived for more than twenty long years as homeless wanderer it must have

---

[1] Mt. Kugami stands in the central part of Niigata Prefecture. It has become well known for its special connection with Ryōkan.

[2] This small hut is known as "Gogō An." It stands halfway up Mt. Kugami.

seemed like a mansion more grand and gorgeous than a palace. The following are some poems he wrote about fixing his abode there.

This small hut known as[2] "Gogō An" where Ryōkan settled down was rotten and decayed from being exposed to wind and rain for too long a time. The hut shown here (p. 6) is the Gogō An II reconstructed in the faithful imitation of the original during the early part of the Taisho era. (1912–26). The Gogō An is often referred to as a grassy hut, wood-log cabin or merely as "his hut," and sometimes humorously as his mansion.

Now Ryōkan lived here for ten years after he came back from his homeless wandering, when he was forty-seven. During these ten years, Ryōkan produced a good number of his masterpieces in the realm of poetry.

1. Inside this lonely hut
   Nothing notable you could find
   Though outside stand
   Innumerable Japanese cedars.

   On the walls are hanging
   Several scrolls of poems
   In high praise of the virtues of Buddha.

   Sometimes dust is found in the pan
   And steam is seldom seen
   To rise out of the steaming basket.

   There lives an old man.
   In a village in the east.

   And he will often knock at the door
   When the moon shines bright.

五合庵
索々五合庵
室如懸磬然
戸外杉千株
壁上偈數篇
釜中時有塵
甑裡更無煙
唯有東村叟
頻叩月下門

2. In the evening dusk
    I often climb up Mt. Kugami
    Treading a mountain-path
    Which leads me on to the peak
    Where I hear some deer
    Plaintively belling.

    And at the foot
    Maples are scattered.
    They are lying quiet;
    Thus silence deepened.
    Now there lie
    The leaves piled thick,
    Calm and serene.

    たそがれに　国上の山を　越えくれば
    　　高嶺には　鹿ぞ啼くなり
    　　麓には　紅葉散りしく
    　　鹿のごと　音にこそ泣かね　もみじ葉の
    　　いやしくしくに　ものぞかなしき
    Tasogare ni　Kugami no yama o　koe kureba
    　　takane ni wa　shika zo nakunari
    　　fumoto ni wa　momiji chirishiku
    　　shika no goto　oto ni koso nakane　momijiba no
    　　iyashikushiku ni　monozo kanashiki

3. Green grow the July grasses
    Running wild all over

And I will stay here in the hut
Yes; in the solitary hut here.

夏草は　心のまゝに　茂りけり
われいほりせむ　これのいほりに
Natsu kusa wa　kokorono mama ni　shigerikeri
ware ihori semu　koreno ihori ni

4. Would that I may grow old
Here in this hut
In the shake of the woods
Covering Mt. Kugami!

いざこゝに　わが身は老いむ　あしびきの
国上の山の　森の下蔭
Iza koko ni　wagami wa oimu　ashibiki no
Kugami no yama no　mori no shitakage

5. Why, coming to the hut "Gogō An"
I see nothing but mountains
Endlessly waving on!

来て見れば　山ばかりなり　五合庵
Kitemireba　yamabakarinari　Gogō An

In former days, in Japan, there were rather many Buddhist
monks and friars who led a secluded life. Some lived among the
remoter mountains and disciplined themselves in a way more

rigid and severe; but most of them fell into oblivion as time passed away. Nor did they have anything to do with the life of the masses. Ryōkan was of different stuff by nature.

He spent a good part of his life among the lonely mountains all by himself leading a simple life. Of course day after day he made the best of each fleeting moment training himself without knowing that he was going through a strict discipline. Living in this way, he came to see clearly how vitally important it is to love others since after all love is best. Just as a pearl is cultured at the cost of the shell itself, he flung his very existence into the greater life of Nature and found his very life being a part of it. Indeed he could whole-heartedly become one with the mountains, rocks, streams, pines, cedars, bushes, or even with the white clouds hovering about the mountaintops. Even the fathomless depth of silence and the awesome magnificence of his surroundings had become dear to him. Putting the whole of things into a nutshell, it may as well be said that his mind had been so much refined and fortified as not to be subdued by the gaunt loneliness of his surroundings until at last he could sublimate himself and stand above the sentient love no matter how profoundly he was attracted by natural beauty or human ties. Indeed *Veritus liberabitis vos* is a dictum that applies to him to a hair. Only those who have successfully given up the egocentric love can reach a spiritual awakening such as he had attained then.

Don't you find something in the following poems that comes on you—one of the fourth voice of poetry (cf. p. 37, *What Is Poetry?* by John Hall Wheellock) ?

6. Among the mountains
   Where even winged birds rarely nestle,
   How I have lived on
   Since I came to live here!

   とぶ鳥も　かよわぬ山の　おくにさへ
   　　住めば住まるゝ　ものにぞありける
   Tobu tori mo　kayowanu yama no　oku ni sae
   　sumeba sumaruru　mononizo arikeru

7. Listening to the silent sound
   Of the moss-covered stream
   I feel myself grow as calm and transparent
   As the soundless sound of the covered current!

   山かげの　石間をつたふ　苔水の
   　　かすかにわれは　すみわたるかも
   Yamakage no　iwama o tsutau　kokemizu no
   　kasuka ni ware wa　sumiwataru kamo

8. How desolate my life here is!
   But how transparent my mind is
   Just as I spend each day
   As it comes and goes!

   わびぬれど　心はすめり　草のいほ
   　　ひと日ひと日を　おくるばかりに

Wabinuredo   kokoro wa sumeri   kusa no iho
   hitohi hitohi o   okuru bakari ni

9. Living alone in the woods
   Where few visitors cast shadows
   How clean and clear I find the moon
   Beaming so quiet in the blue!

とふ人も　なき山里に　いほりして
　ながむる月の　影ぞくまなき
Touhito mo   naki yamazato ni   ihorishite
   nagamuru tsuki no   kagezo kumanaki

Being human, he would once in a while feel the sting of
hunger; he would set to the village at the foot of the mountain to
go about begging for his food. He knew what hard labor the
farmers had to bear, so he thanked them from the bottom of his
heart even for one handful of rice holding it up reverentially on
his palms. The villagers too, felt happy and offered him with a
good grace what they had raised, as Ryōkan was loved and much
respected by the whole village.

To him the best friends were the village children. He would
often play with them the whole day long enjoying hide-and-seek
and ball-bouncing. What is interesting about this connection is
that he did not play with them because he was forced to but did
so simply because he just loved them.

There are some episodes told of him. Most of them are cen-
tered on his relations with children. In a word, he was a man who
never forgot the joys of childhood.

Below are translated some of his poems and they show how happy he was when he was playing with the children.

10. When a long winter is over,
    I must go down to the village
    To ask for rice from the villagers.
    Then on the road
    I see the children bouncing balls
    Freely enjoying the fragrance of spring,
    "Calling out loud, One, two, three, four, five, six."
    I sing the rhymes for them
    And they bounce balls
    Timing to my singing and vice versa.
    When we stop playing
    The long, hazy spring day
    Has finally come to an end!

冬ごもり春さり来れば飯乞ふと草の庵を立ちいでて里に行けば玉鉾の道の巷に子供らが今を春べと手まりつくひふみよいむな、汝がつけば吾はうたい、あがつけばなは歌ひつきて数へて霞たつ長き春日を暮しつるかも

Fuyugomori haru sarikureba iikou to kusano ihori o tachiidete sato ni yukeba tamaboko no michi no chimata ni kodomoraga ima o harube to temari tsuku hi fu mi yo i mu na, nagatsukeba a wa utai, agatsukeba na wa utai, tsukite kazoete kasumi tatsu, nagaki haruhi o kurashi tsurukamo.

11. Indeed a long, hazy spring day
    Has gone away at last,

As I forgot myself playing with the children
Bouncing balls and singing songs.

霞立つ　長き春日を　子供らと
　　手まりつきつゝ　今日もくらしつ

Kasumi tatsu　nagaki harubi o　kodomo ra to
　temari tsukitsutsu　kyō mo kurashitsu

12. How I wish the day would never end
　　When I play with the children
　　Bouncing balls on and on
　　On a long, long spring day!

子供らと　手まりつきつゝ　此の里に
　　遊ぶ春日は　くれずともよし

Kodomo ra to　temari tsukitsutsu　kono sato ni
　asobu harubi wa　kurezutomo yoshi

13. Ah, how happy I am
　　To go out in the fields
　　And gather tender herbs running about
　　With the merry, merry village children!

子供らと　手たづさわりて　春の野の
　　若菜をつめば　楽しくもあるかな

Kodomo ra to　te tazusawarite　haru no no no
　wakana o tsumeba tanoshiku mo aru kana

In a notebook left behind by Ryōkan, the following entries

are found. Reading it, we can realize how he was getting along everyday—so simply and frugally. In the worn-out notebook are mentioned a hood, a towel, some paper, a fan, some money, a bouncing ball, and some marbles. Just think of him having mentioned a bouncing ball and marbles in his notebook. How fascinated he was by these past times! Of course in those days, there were no rubber balls; it would have been too luxurious a thing. It was a hand-made ball with some figures spun on it with colored threads. He was very fond of playing marbles, too. Once he was found joyfully playing marbles with a geisha girl and was reprimanded for doing so as it was too undisciplined a thing for him—a Buddhist monk!

In fact he must have been eccentric in a sense. For example, he had a strong tendency to believe what others would not have believed—that is to say, what they said for jokes. Isn't this what commonly prevails among children? There were similarities in the mental activity of Ryōkan and of children at least to some extent. Anyway the whole village, especially the village children, would always be waiting for him to come down to the village whenever spring came. It is natural that he should have been loved by the whole village, such a good-natured man to the bone! We must firmly be in the grip of this character of his for we believe this is an important clue to the real understanding of his unique character.

His pen name was Taigu (a great fool). He was really too good-natured—if not a fool. How difficult it is to find such a man in the world of today teeming with so many self-made VIPs!

His Buddhist master, Kokusen (1722–91) said of him: "Ryōkan looks like a fool; but his way of life was an entirely emancipated one. He lives on playing, so to say, with his destiny, liberating himself from every kind of fetter." He breathed the same breath with the autumn splendor with which the whole mountain was ablaze even while he was sleeping.

One of his fellow monks, Tainin (1781?–1811) also said of him:

> He willingly got rid of everything either material or mental, thus sublating himself above the phenomenal. He looks like a fool or an idiot. He does not live in the ever-changing phenomenal world even though he mingles with the shrewd people ready to exploit others, nor is he captured by good and evil. In the morning he wanders out of his hut and goes God knows where and in the evening loiters around somewhere. For fame he cares nothing. Men's cunning ways he puts out of the question. Once he came to see me and told me something mysterious. When I had been ill in bed for a long time he kept on taking care of me till I was completely cured. Really I owe so much to him. How can I pay back the genuine kindness he has constantly shown to me?

The following is the certificate given to Ryōkan by his Buddhist master, Kokusen, in 1970.

> Ryo, foolish though you look, now you've found a very wide but true path, which few people can get to. In celebration of your accomplishment, you shall have

this walking stick. It looks plain but it's not. Go, go, in peace. Now the whole world is your residence. With this stick leaning against any wall, you might have a good slumber.

14. Ever since I saw the light
I have set at naught the worldly glories,
Leaving my destiny to chance.
In my bag remains only three bushels of rice;
And beside the hearth lies only one bundle of firewood.
Who should worry about salvation or retribution?
Fame and fortune are only so much dust!
At night, when it rains, I stretch out my limbs,
And fall asleep soundly—
Though my mansion is a small, small hut in the woods.

生涯懶立身
騰々任天真
囊中三升米
爐邊一束薪
誰問迷悟跡
何知名利塵
夜雨草庵裡
雙脚等間伸

15. Here in this hut on the hill
I have lived day and night
Caring nothing—not even for the mold
That covers the lips nor for the ash

That falls on my head. I would only
Sit in meditation in this hut of mine;
I have already forsaken the wordly fame,
Much less do I care for my appearance
That may reflect in the mirror.
Indeed stranger and outsider am I
To the world's approbation and condemnation!

千峰一草堂
終身粗布衣
任生口邊醭
懶掃頭上灰
己無銜花鳥
何有當鏡台
無心逐流俗
信人呼癡獸

16. I know not
How many springs and winters
Have I passed in this solitary hut
Since I began to stay in it.
And all these years, I have lived on
The eatable weeds, the rice and vegetables,
I have made it a habit to beg at the villagers'
And happy at being left alone
I'm satisfied with
Living among the woods.

Especially since I returned from the journey
I'm enjoying my own life.

坐　還　未　偏　米　菜　不　幽
臥　來　厭　喜　自　只　知　樓
任　殊　林　人　乞　藜　幾　地
屈　疏　下　事　比　藿　冬　從
伸　慵　貧　少　隣　是　春　占

17. What is it to live?
Well, for a while, let me just keep on living
As I have done so far.
Let me laugh when I am inclined to;
Let me shed tears when I am sad!
Indeed, I am neither for the world nor against it.
Outside a fine spring rain is falling endlessly
And yet the straw rugs have not been lightened yet
By the blooming plum blossoms.
All through the morning I sit around the hearth,
Having none to talk with.
Then I reach my arms for some folding copy books
At my back to practise calligraphy.

此生何所似
騰々且任緣
堪笑兮堪嘆
非俗非沙門
蕭々春雨裡
庭梅未照筵
終朝圍爐坐
相對也無言
背手探法帖
薄云供幽閒

Ryōkan says "I am neither for the world nor against it." In these words we can see how unique he could be. He could not put up with those who would go pretending. How he abhorred to pretend to be a monk! Indeed, he could not and would not bear with the sermons of professional preachers.

In those days, the best means to get along either from the viewpoint of living a respectable life or from that of merely making livelihood was to own a temple and live there as chief-priest. But he had always kept himself aloof from worldly success. He had been too well acquainted with the empty life inside a big temple. He was familiar with the fruitless life in a seemingly posperous temple and positively tried hard to live up to his own deep life-philosophy, even going so far as to give up every chance to lead an ordinary monk's life, to say nothing of a luxurious one.

Indeed he was a man, so to say, who willingly led a most frugal yet joyful life in sheer poverty. He paid little attention to how the world would treat him. He may have looked on himself rather as a black sheep in his family as well as in the outside world. He must have thought that he had no excuse to beg anything from the hardworking farmers. Once in a while, he may have wondered why he should continue to live as he had. On a cold, freezing night, sitting alone in his hut he must have meditated on and on. But for the meditation he might have been frozen or starved to death.

The following is a poem in which he expressed himself as candidly as possible.

18. Oh, my three-mat room;
How old and miserable I have grown!
I am quite at a loss how to describe
The painful experiences I have had night after night
During the coldest season—patiently looking forward
To the advent of spring.
Unless I beg some more rice, how can I keep
My body and soul together? At this stage,
No matter how deeply I may meditate,
I find that it helps me no more
As a means to support my life.
Now, I will compose poems for the deceased
To while away the tedious hours.

書	靜	何	不	數	啜	辛	況	摧	蕭
詩	思	以	乞	日	粥	苦	方	殘	条
寄	無	凌	斗	遲	消	具	玄	朽	三
故	活	此	升	陽	寒	難	冬	老	間
人	計	辰	米	春	夜	陳	節	身	屋

Here a short description of the society in which he lived may help you understand why he had chosen to live at such a secluded spot.

In those days, the Tokugawa shogunate government (1603–1867) was ruling the whole country, and it was one of the most gloomy periods in Japan's history. Injustice and cruelty prevailed everywhere, and a long continued draught, terrible storms, the prevalence of epidemics, and a series of severe earthquakes, culminating in the great earthquake of the Ansei era (1854–60) added to the misery of the people. As for Ryōkan himself, four years after he renounced the world and became a wandering monk, he lost his mother. In memory of his mother he composed the following poem:

19. In the morning and evening,
     I look far away over the sea
     Looking upon the Island of Sado
     As my angel mother's memento!

     たらちねの　母がかたみと　朝夕に
     佐渡の島べを　うち見つるかも
     Tarachine no　haha ga katami to　asa yū ni
     Sado no shimabe o　uchi mitsurukamo

Again about ten years later, his father passed away. He is said to have thrown himself into the Katsura River near Kyoto. He was a rather well-known haiku poet, and had been indignant about the corrupt world and full of passion for reforming it, but what he had planned to do remained only a blueprint to the last.

He was driven to the wall at last and threw himself into the river. His father's sudden death was an irrevocable blow to Ryōkan.

20. With the tears overflowing my eyes
     Father's graceful handwritings grow dim
     As I read them on
     Calling to mind my dear father!

  みずぐきの　跡も涙に　かすみけり
　　在りし昔の　ことを想ひて
  Mizuguki no   ato mo namida ni   kasumi keri
  arishi mukashi no koto o omoite

Remembering the past now gone for good, and the piercing solitude surrounding him in and out, his only solace was found in composing poems, some of which are shown below:

21. My sleeves are wet with tears
     Brooding on the ups and downs
     Of which so full is the world
     As it goes shifting on and on!

  わが袖は　しとどにぬれぬ　うつせみの
　　うき世のなかの　ことをおもふに
  Waga sode wa   shitodo ni nurenu   utsusemi no
  ukiyo no naka no   koto o omouni

22. Heavy as the burdens are
     For the world to carry,

How could I bear them all
Even in my bosom?

諸人の　かこつおもひを　せきとめて
　おのれひとりに　しらしめんとか
Morobito no　kakotsu omoi o　sekitomete
　onore hitori ni　shirashimen to ka

23. What a fragile gossamer-like existence I am!
The more I think of this
The more keenly I begin to feel
My own transiency!

わがことや　はかなきものは　またもあらじと
　おもへばいよよ　はかなかりけり
Waga koto ya　hakanaki mono wa　matamo araji to
　omoeba iyoyo　hakanakarikeri

24. How deeply I am concerned
With the sorrows of the world
And as often am I
Quite at a loss what to do!

世の中を　おもひおもひて　はてはては
　いかにやいかに　ならむとすらむ
Yononaka o　omoi omoite　hate hate wa
　ika ni ya ika ni　naramu to suramu

25. Some people will give up
    Even their life to save the world
    And yet how can I enjoy myself
    Living as I am in this grassy hut?

身をすてゝ　世を救ふ人も　ますものを
草のいほりに　ひまもとむとは

Mi o sutete   yo o sukuu hito mo   masu mono o
kusa no ihori ni   hima motomu to wa

Ryōkan had a famous pedigree; generation after generation of his ancestors held the hereditary post of a Shintō priest. As he had deserted his home to become a wandering monk, the heirship was turned over to his younger brother. In the meantime, his family became involved in a troublesome affair with a powerful rich man in a neighboring village which developed into a lawsuit, resulting in the loss of the whole property of Ryōkan's household.

Taking these circumstances into consideration, there was nothing left for him but to keep going along the way he had chosen. Indeed he was always on the go—in some sense.

Winter in the north of Japan is always severe and lasts long. Of course then he found it hardly possible to go to the village at the foot of Mt. Kugami to ask for rice.

As a rule no one would come to see him since around his hut everything lay buried under the snow. The water streaking down from the back hill was the only sign and source of life for him. Here are some poems Ryōkan composed while he was living in such surroundings:

26. Confining myself to the snow-covered hut
    On the slope of Mt. Kugami,
    I have had none to call on me
    It has snowed all day and all night long.
    No trace of human creatures is left now, not
    Even their shadows appear here. Indeed, only
    The mountain stream, winding like a straw-rope
    Among the rocks and pebbles, has been supporting
    My life up to this very moment!

あしびきの国上の山の冬ごもり、日に日に雪のふるなべに
行き来の道の跡もたえ、故さと人の音もなし
うき世をこゝに門さして、ひだのたくみがうつ縄の
唯一すじの岩清水
そのいのちにてあらたまのことしのけふも
くらしつるかも

Ashibiki no Kugami no yama no fuyugomori, hi ni hi ni yuki no
    furunabe ni
yukiki no michi no atomo tae, furusatobito no oto mo nashi
ukiyo o koko ni kado sashi te, hida no takumi ga utsunawa no
tada hitosuji no iwashimizu
sono inochi nite aratama no kotoshi no kyō mo kurashi
    tsurukamo

27. No rippling of the mountain stream
    Is heard among the rocks;
    Maybe the thick snow is falling
    Over the peaks towering high.

さよふけて岩間の滝つ音せぬは
　　高ねのみ雪ふりつもるらし

Sayofuke te iwama no takitsu oto senu wa

takane no miyuki furi tsumoru rashi

28. My "home" stands on Mt. Kugami
   A solitary hut deep among the woods
   And during the months of winter
   None would dare come up here.

わがいほは、国上やまもと　ふゆごもり
　　ゆきゝの人の　あとさえぞなき

Waga iho wa, Kugami yamamoto　fuyugomori

yukiki no hito no　ato sae zo naki

29. How can I tell the floating world
   The penetrating loneliness of a lonely man
   Living in a solitary hut all by himself
   During the long silent winter night ?

柴の戸の　ふゆのゆふべのさびしさを
　　うき世の人に　いかで語らむ

Shiba no to no　fuyu no yūbe no sabishisa o

ukiyo no hito ni　ikade kataramu

30. I haven't been even to the village
   Wandering out there begging rice
   Since it has been snowing on and on
   Day after day.

飯乞ふと　里にもいでず　なりにけり
きのふもけふも　雪のふれゝば
Ii kou to　sato ni mo idezu　nari ni keri
kinou mo kyō mo　yuki no furereba

31. When the snow lies thick
    Wrapping up my solitary hut
    Even my soul I feel vanishing
    As evening dusk gathers thick!

み山びの　雪ふりつもる　夕ぐれは
わが心さへ　消ぬべくおもほゆ
Miyamabi no　yuki furi tsumoru　yūgure wa
waga kokoro sae　kenubeku omo hoyu

How desperately forlorn he must have felt while sitting alone in the hut enshrouded in the white winding sheet of snow! For rather a long time even the mountain stream had stopped sounding. Indeed how many of us could stand such overwhelming loneliness!

One may question us: "Why should he escape the world that much and that far?" People may attack him, saying "Does his way of living all alone have anything to do with the happiness of the people in general?" For thirty long years, he lived all alone. Why? Read the following poems and you will find some clue as you peek into his inner life.

32. How can I live a true man's life
    Treading the path of righteousness

Even for a single day
Out of one thousand days?

いかにして　まことの道に　かなひなむ
　　千とせのうちの　一日なりとも

Ikani shite　makoto no michi ni　kanai namu
　　chitose no uchi no　hitohi nari tomo

33. Whether awake or asleep
I have been yearning to go ahead
Along the way for the true
No matter how hard it is.

いかにして　まことの道に　かなはんと
　　ひとへにおもふ　ねてもさめても

Ikani shite　makoto no michi ni　kanawan to
　　hitoe ni omou　nete mo samete mo

When young he is said to have planned to found a leper
house or go to China to study Buddhism there. But these plans
had no chance to be realized. Then, coming to this pass he found
only one way to go: he made up his mind, to go his own way,
that is to say, to pursue the way of truth—the only way a true
man can follow, believing that by doing so, he may turn himself
into a light, be it ever so little and dim, yet bright enough to urge
a helpless traveler to go even a few more steps forward.

He had come to find no discrimination between 'you and I'.
In him, 'you' and 'I' are one and the same. After all, he could
sublimate himself into the transphenomenal region. In other

words, he had come to find the more spacious vista opening before him. He jumped into the wide expanding life that makes every creature and everything alive with the ever-bounding-forward life-force.

At the same time he could not help loving the whole world both visible and invisible. In the *Eiheiroku* by Dōgen (1200–54), a famous Buddhist abbot, he found a chapter entitled "Love Words." He copied it faithfully and always kept it on hand.

* * *

Love Words
—From the *Eiheiroku* (永平録)—

Love Words should always be used when we keep company with others. We should not utter violent words. With the people in general it is an important etiquette to greet them with the polite and sincere wishes for their good health.

Among the Buddhist priests, there prevails a custom to inquire after their health feeling grateful for one another. And again they are to love their parents telling nothing of it to others.

When we speak to others in genuine love-expressions such as we use to our babies, we are practicing the love words. Let us praise the virtuous; let us show pity to the virtueless. When we are anxious to give the love words, their enlivening power will gradually expand. Then will come forth such precious love words as are usually hidden from us so long as we remain indifferent strangers to them.

When we use the love words while we live in this world of ours, we shall be adamantine to any change of destiny. Even a deadly foe will be made to yield by the power of love words; still more, perfect harmony will come to be realized with the virtuous people.

When we hear people speak the love words, we feel calm and peaceful both within and without.

When we hear them spoken for the people having no chance to speak face to face, they will take root in the deeper part of our inner life.

Indeed the love words come straight out of the love mind, which is no less than the reflection of benevolent pity. We should learn that the love words sincerely given have the power to transfer a big mountain to the sea. But only to appreciate a person's ability does not have this much effect."

Evidently the love words must have had a lasting influence on Ryōkan. In this respect we find the following interesting or even fascinating since Ryōkan himself is speaking plainly through these poems:

34. On a beautiful day in spring
    I went out into an eastern village,
    Sounding the silver rings on my staff.
    The willows around the pond had grown
    Smoky with the green foliage and
    On the pond were floating some water plants.
    In my bowl was the rice, token of the people's best wishes
    And my heart was full of heavenly riches
    Making me feel even like standing
    Far above the highest ranks!
    Thus I went pilgrimaging from place to place

Where some sages of the past had once lived
Relying on the people's love and the Heart of Buddha.

春氣　稍和調　錫を鳴して東城に出ず

青々たり　園中の柳　泛々たり池上の萍

鉢は香し　千家の飯　心に拠つ万乗の榮

古佛の跡を追慕して　次第に食を乞うて行く

At one time, Ryōkan spoke about Abbot Senkei, his master-priest, as follows:

> Abbot Senkei is truly a virtuous man in the genuine sense of the word. He is a man of few words and does not pretend to himself. He has been staying in a temple at Kokusen for twenty years but I have neither known him attending a religious meditation nor seen him read a Buddhist scripture. None have I heard him give a sermon. He always grows vegetables to give them to a wandering monk. I have known him for rather a long time without knowing what he really is. I really wish I could meet him now in person, but how can I? He must have been one of those rare men who are always closely united with the spirit of Buddha.

Kera (1810–60), who was a good friend of Ryōkan's, left behind a notebook. This notebook helps us much in understanding what kind of man Ryōkan was. The following is a quotation from the notebook:

My master (Ryōkan) has never been heard to speak about the scriptures at home or abroad nor have I ever heard him urge others to do good for one another. Time and again he gathers dead leaves of which a bonfire is made or sits at meditation in the temple hall. I have never heard him quote any poem or a literary work while talking with others nor even a single example by way of urging others to go in the virtuous way. To be showy is an entirely foreign element in his daily life, he is simply living like a speck of white cloud sailing across the blue expanse. Indeed, one may turn out to be a virtuous man only through coming in contact with such a man.

By and by more and more people came to visit him and he too called on some people who stood on good terms with him. One evening he found he had left behind his staff as he was on his way back from the house of a friend of his to his mountain hut. Just then he composed a short poem which runs as follows:

35. None could read
    How sad an old man could be
    As I was homeward wending
    Missing my staff in the dusk.

老が身の　あわれを誰に　語らまし
杖を忘れて　帰る夕暮

Oi ga mi no   aware o tare ni   katara mashi
tsue o wasure te   kaeru yūgure

Needless to say, no one was waiting for him in his mountain hut. Sometimes on his way home he found himself having an irresistible impulse to speak to the pine trees at the roadside. The following are some of the poems he composed at such moments.

36. Could the pine trees speak
    Standing on the hill at dusk
    I would ask of them
    The things of the by gone days

夕ぐれの　岡の松の木　人ならば
　昔のことを　問はましものを
Yūgure no   oka no matsunoki   hito naraba
　mukashi no koto o   towamashi mono o

37. Ah, Lonely Pine, on the lonely mountain,
    Were you a living creature,
    You might put on my sedge-hat and straw-coat
    To shift on in the rain.

ひとつ松　人にありせば　笠かさましを
　蓑きせましを　ひとつ松あはれ
Hitotsu matsu   hito ni ariseba   kasa kasamashi o
　Mino kise mashi o   hitotsu matsu aware

For him who had no family of his own, every vessel and

utensil, poor and meager as it was, had become his dear partner. A mashing bowl was the hardest worker. It was used as a vessel for making miso soup and he would often use the bowl for a water bucket, carrying back pure water in it from a mountain stream. Again he had to wash his face and hands using the same. But he found his best friend in his bowl, with which he always went to beg for rice. He always accepted rice in it. Neither on a scorching hot day nor on a freezing cold day did he ever part with it. When he heard rice grains rustling into it, he could not help but feel himself full of gratitude for the warm human heart that must have been poured into the bowl together with the rice. He would often hold it high with his hands to show his unalloyed gratitude. The rice and vegetables thus given to him could keep him alive.

And indeed it was this very bowl which he had made so much of that he once forgot to bring back after playing with the village children, leaving it lying on the grass. He had become that absent-minded! The following two poems clearly express how keenly he missed the bowl.

38. How I miss Hachinoko (his begging bowl)
    I left behind at the roadside
    While gathering violet flowers!
    Where does it lie now, my Hachinoko?

道のべに　菫つみつゝ鉢の子を
　　忘れてぞ来し　亜はれ鉢の子
Michinobe ni　sumire tsumi tsutsu hachi no ko o
　wasure te zo koshi　aware hachi no ko

39. Alas, I was so forgetful
    That I left behind my Hachinoko.
    No one, I hope, will take it away;
    Oh, my dear Hachinoko!
    No, none will dare!

    鉢の子を　わが忘るれども　とる人はなし
    　　取る人はなし　あはれ鉢の子
    Hachi no ko o　waga wasurure domo　toru hito wa nashi
    　　toru hito wa nashi　aware hachi no ko

When the lights began to glimmer in the distance even the beasts of the woods longed for their parents and the long drawn sound of the bells of the temple on Mt. Kugami would often waft on the evening breeze. At such moments, he composed the following poems.

40. At dusk, I was going over the hill
    Watching leaves falling fast; but
    I feel my fingers turning numb
    Though warming them in the robe-sleeves.

    夕暮に　国上の山を　越えくれば
    　　衣手寒し　木の葉散りつゝ
    Yūgure ni　Kugami no yama o　koe kureba
    　　koromode samushi　konoha chiri tsutsu

41. How I longed for a companion
    To share this piercing lonesomeness,

When I was coming home at nightfall
Carrying some herbs in my basket!

山住みの　あはれを　誰に　語らまし
　　あかざ籠に入れ　かへる夕ぐれ
Yamazumi no   aware o   tare ni   katara mashi
　　akaza kago ni ire   kaeru yūgure

The herbs he gathered were the pigweeds he usually ate for supper.

He was a good dancer. He was in his own element when enjoying a dance after drinking saké with his friends. Can't you feel his buoyancy in the following lines ?

42. O, the wind blows so clean
And the moon shines so clear;
Let us dance on all through the night
Though my days are numbered!

風はきよし　月はさやけし　いざともに
　　踊り明かさむ　老のなごりに
Kaze wa kiyoshi   tsuki wa sayakeshi   iza tomoni
　　odori akasamu   oi no nagori ni

43. How can I sleep tonight
When the moon beams so bright?
Dear friends, let us sing together
As I will dance all night through.

いざ歌へ　われ立ち舞はむ　ひさかたの
　こよひの月に　寝ねらるべしや

Iza utae　ware tachi mawamu　hisakata no
　koyoi no tsuki ni　inerarubeshi ya

44. I know not what awaits me tomorrow
    Nor what will become of me hereafter
    But for today better forget every care
    Quaffing nectar cup after cup!

あすよりの　後のよすがは　いざしらず
　今日のひと日は　酔ひにけらしも

Asu yori no　nochi no yosuga wa　iza shirazu
　kyō no hitohi wa　yoi ni kerashimo

When these friends were leaving, he usually saw them off escorting them along the winding mountain path. Read the following poems, and you will sense what kind of man he was.

45. May the beaming moon
    Shine on clean and clear
    Since my friends are leaving
    And the path is strewn with nuts.

月よみの　光を待ちて　帰りませ
　山路は栗の　いがの多きに

Tsuki yomi no　hikari o machi te　kaeri mase
　yamaji wa kuri no　iga no ōki ni

Once, when the green breeze carried the sounds of merry-making from the village at the foot of the mountain, he composed the following:

46. In the village
    Are sounding drums and flutes;
    But here on the mountain
    Only the pines are whispering.

里べには　笛や太鼓の　音すなり
深山はさはに　松の音して

Satobe ni wa　fue ya taiko no　oto sunari
miyama wa sawa ni　matsu no oto shite

When he left his hut he was nearly seventy. It had become too much for him to climb up and down the rugged and winding mountain paths day after day. He passed away in 1828 in a small room attached to the house of one of his best friends. He was seventy-four. From that time, for a very long time, his hut was exposed to wind and rain, until at last it rotted away.

Now the Gogō An II has been built where the first one used to stand, and a block of stone has been placed there as a monument. You will find inscribed on it a representative haiku.

47. Ah, how a wind
    Brings in
    Dead leaves just enough
    As I burn them on!

たく程は　風が持てくる　落葉かな
Taku hodo wa　kaze ga mote kuru　ochiba kana

Another haiku (supposedly not his own but he loved it and murmured it at his last moment).

48. Each maple leaf,
    Fluttering away,
    One and all,
    Showing its face and back.

裏を見せ　表を見せて　散るもみじ
Ura o mise　omote o misete　chiru momiji

Some short poems equally impressive are translated below:

49. The wide, wide universe
    Stands silent in the snow
    And in it is falling
    The light snow still!

あは雪の　中に立ちたる　三千大千
　またその中に　あは雪ぞふる
*Awayuki no　naka ni tachi taru　michiōchi
　mata sono naka ni　awayuki zo furu*

50. What shall I leave as my mementos:
    Flowers in spring

Mountain cuckoos in summer
And in autumn, crimson maples?

形見とて　何かのこさむ　春は花
　山ほととぎす　秋はもみじ葉
Katami tote　nanika nokosamu　haru wa hana
　yama-hototogisu　aki wa momijiba

51. When we are to meet a calamity
The best way to avoid calamity is just to confront it.
When the time to die has come,
The best way is to meet death.
This is the panacea for us
To dodge a calamity.

These poems together with others are most expressive of his
satori (spiritual awakening or enlightenment).

• • •

Here it is not out of place to touch upon what has made the
memories of Ryōkan so precious and so fond to us Japanese.
Furthermore, through coming in contact with his life we are led
to true understanding of a unique personality and may be led on
to gain at least some glimpses of Zen awakening. We may not be
able to point out this or that as an example of the life of a Zen
monk, but in his daily life you may find some phases that might
be taken as an example of the life of a Zen monk or a deeply
awakened layman thoroughly disciplined by the spirit of Zen.

Ryōkan's life was filled with so many episodes—some are very familiar with us. These episodes clearly and even sympathetically show us what kind of man he was. Indeed, a man's true personality is often more clearly and naturally revealed in the episodes told of him, though after all they may turn out to be nothing but episodes.

One day, when he was a mere boy, he did something that hurt his father's feelings. He was severely reprimanded by his father. Then Eizō (Ryōkan's childhood name) stared at his father from the corners of his eyes so steadily and unflinchingly that his father grew all the more angry and exasperated until at last he exclaimed, "If you stare at me so, you will change yourself into a flatfish." Needless to say, his father did not mean anything serious by this; but Eizō took the malediction seriously. All at once he stole out of the house, away to the beach, without telling anything to anyone, and climbed on top of a rock facing the rough sea washing the shores of northern Japan, constantly breaking on the cold gray stones.

By and by the whole family found that Eizō was missing and they all went out, each carrying a paper lantern, to look for the missing boy. They searched after him—leaving no stone unturned. Finally a boy was found sitting still on a rock—focusing his gaze upon the sea. And this boy was none other than the missing Eizō himself!

The first thing they heard him say was, "Haven't I changed into a flatfish yet?" He must have been looking over the sea believing himself to be changing into a flatfish. How childish and how simple he was! But this perfect innocence, for which you might reasonably look upon him as a mysterious creature standing on the rim of stupidity, was one of the dominant forces that had acted as a decisive element in critical moments throughout his life.

He was born as heir to a famous family, but he left home as a wandering monk when he was around twenty-two and went through so many peculiar and hard experiences for more than twenty years. But why he did so is beyond our understanding as we have no reliable sources to enlighten us concerning this part of his life.

After wandering as a monk for so long a time, he came back to a spot not so far from his birthplace and finally settled down at a small hut located half way up Mt. Kugami in Niigata Prefecture in the northern part of Japan. It was chiefly while living here all by himself that he lived a life full of peerless experiences, both spiritual and physical, which blended with his tissue to be filtered through deep meditations into an element which caused him to become loftier, more exquisite, and yet tough. Some of these experiences which must have contributed very much to his spiritual awakening were so severe and rigorous they would have made others drop away.

He was living quite an independent life in a small grassy hut among the pines and cedars always lonely and alone in close touch with the *genus loci* or the spirit of the mountain. While living in this way, whenever he had an inspirational urge, he composed short poems (sometimes longer ones, too, in Chinese). And in these poems we may come across some lines or phrases clearly expressive of his process of spiritual awakening—especially in the poems he composed in the acute loneliness, which came keenly and nakedly upon him from time to time.

There was a village at the foot of Mt. Kugami he often visited. He could not but feel unbearably lonesome when he saw the glimmering lights in the village of an autumn evening—though he could remain calm enough to objectively observe himself in such a situation and to compose some of his most impressive poems touching his deepest philosophical interpretation of human life. Indeed he seemed to have been able to merge imperceptibly into his surroundings so that he could share the same atmosphere with the cedar woods where his mountain hut was nestled and also with many folds of mountains waving on endlessly. And yet being a warm-hearted person, time and again he had a strong longing for human intercourse when the heart-devouring loneliness was closing in upon him from all sides. To Ryōkan, the flights of wild geese flying far up in the moon-lit sky, a deer belling and calling his mate in the woods, the stream silently running among and under the moss-covered rocks, the whole mountain ablaze with autumnal glories and the deep snow covering mountain after mountain like a big white carpet spreading on and on were none other than the expression of the cosmic life-rhythm pervading the whole universe. Why could he come to have this kind of spiritual awakening? It is no less than the result of his having perfectly melted into the core of what he had grasped as the Cosmic Life. In other words, he had a keen sense of the spiritual harmony between him and the whole universe.

It is said that the essence of Zen consists in attaining *satori* (spiritual awakening or enlightenment) and we believe he had a number of strong motivations for attaining *satori* especially during these ten years he had spent on Mt. Kugami. In this connection, what we should not forget is that he had freely expressed his mind in his poems by means of which we may gradually approach the heart of his *satori,* though he had never tried openly to speak about it. It is emanating out of his poems in varied nuances like a river flowing on taking various courses. Whenever we read some of his poems, we can hardly do so without being deeply impressed by his personality, ever progressive and creative.

Jesus says, "Unless you turn round and become like children, you will never enter the Kingdom of Heaven." (Luke 18:17). Ryōkan kept on cherishing the innocent childlike mind throughout his life and in this respect, he is quite unique. We could compare him to Tolstoy's *Ivan the Fool,* published in 1868.

Everything or every creature was dear to him—from his ever-useful begging bowl he could never part from to a little murmuring stream trickling through the mossy rocks. Indeed he was grateful for everything. The following poems will tell you something definite about his conception of life, which oozes out of the depths of his inward life.

52. A lone pine stands
    In the fields of Iwamuro
    And how miserably soaked
    It was in the rain.
    When I looked at it today.
    Oh, Solitary Pine,
    How gladly would I have
    Protected you with my paper-umbrella
    Or with my straw-coat
    Were you only flesh and blood.
    What a pity—to see you drenched so!

岩室の　田中に立てる
ひとつ松の木　けふ見れば
しぐれの雨に　ねれつゝ立てり
ひとつ松　人にありせば
笠　貸さましを　蓑　着せましを
ひとつ松　あはれ

Iwamuro no   tanaka ni tateru

hitotsu matsu no ki   kyō mireba

shigure no ame ni   nuretsutsu tateri

hitotsu matsu   hito ni ariseba

kasa   kasamashi o   mino   kisemashi o

hitotsu matsu   aware

The same innocent mind that made the young Eizō feel like changing into a flatfish when reprimanded by his father is transparently revealed in his whole-hearted attachment to the drenched pine.

Here is another example that goes as far in showing what he was. One night a burglar broke into his hut. The burglar must have been a total stranger, for if not, how could he have thought of breaking into the hut since the master of the hut was living there poorer than a mouse in a deserted church. He should have known this much at least. After the burglar left the hut, Ryōkan came back and looked up at the calmly shining moon. On the spur of the moment, he composed the following:

53. Hi, Moon,
    You were left behind
    By the gentleman of the road

While peeping in
Through the window!

ぬす人に　取り残されし　窓の月
Nusubito ni　torinokosareshi　mado no tsuki

At one time, it may have been toward the end of October, a beggar came to his hut and asked for something but as he had nothing to give since his robe had already been taken away. Though winter had not come yet, he felt chilly. Then he composed the following, warmly calling to mind the beggar:

54. Where is he wandering
    Sleeping wherever he's destined to,
    No matter how awkwardly chilly a night wind
    And how completely dark, the night ?

    いずこにか　旅ねしつらむ　ぬばたまの
    夜半のあらしの　うたてさむきに
    *Izuko ni ka　tabine shitsuramu　nubatama no
    yowa no arashi no　utate samuki ni*

Mt. Kugami, where his hut stood, was situated in the northern part of Japan, rather notorious for severe cold. That he could live on just by himself so calmly that no matter what might befall him he could always keep himself standing above the phenomenal—that after all he had reached this stage must have been due to the genuine *satori* he had wisely acquired, through passing various disciplinary stages motivated by his everyday life.

The episodes given in the following pages clearly show his unique character, too.

In a village close to Mt. Kugami, there lived a ferry boatman. He was widely known for being too ready to resort to violence in dealing with the villagers. This man had often become irritated at Ryōkan's gentle and kind manners and at last he made up his mind to stir him up to anger. One day he deliberately led Ryōkan on to his boat and when the boat had reached half-way down the river, he caused the boat to pitch and roll violently until at last Ryōkan, who was like an anvil in the water, was thrown overboard into the river. Of course he had a very hard time of it. The boatman was shocked to find Ryōkan struggling for life as he could scarcely keep his head above the water. On seeing Ryōkan in this plight, even the ill-natured boatman lost no time in pulling the drenched monk out of the water. Then Ryōkan also lost no time in thanking the boatman for saving his life!

Ryōkan had made some extract out of the *Butsui Kyōkyō* (a kind of Buddhist scripture) which he always kept on hand. The following is a passage he loved best:

> You, monks and nuns, even though some one attacks you with the grapes of wrath you should carefully try to compose yourself and never get stirred to anger. You should guard your mouth and never allow it to utter bad words. If you should indulge yourself in name-calling, you will prevent the Buddha's Benevolence from spreading out and the true virtues will be stunted and die away. Indeed patience is a great

virtue. Compared with this, any form of special discipline will be of no avail. When you practice patience,
you will be treading the path for a true man of virtue.
If you will not hear others speak ill of you with a good
grace and joy, tasting it as if you were sipping sweet
wine, you would be falling far short of being a man of
true wisdom. Why does it pull you down so low?
Because then you would destroy your noble quality.
Nobody will feel an inner urge to do good when he
sees such a man in the days to come. We must go far
enough to understand that anger is more destructive
than a great conflagration. Indeed we should seriously
try to guard ourselves against the evil powers. After all
the most vicious thief to steal the real virtues is, needless to say, "being stirred to anger."

It is not so difficult to preach but how hard it is to put into
practice what we preach. Ryōkan did preach very little, if any, but
he was always ready to do whatever he could for others. In this his
attractive personality shines beautifully. Neither did he strive nor
hustle nor pretend but just loved others as naturally as water flows
down a mountain or a white cloud sails on in the expanse. He
was supremely peerless in this connection. Isn't this because he
would often be led by the spirit of Zen?

Ryōkan was in his own element when he was playing with
the village children. Of all games, ball-bouncing and playing marbles he liked best of all.

It was said that he was always carrying a ball and some marbles in his begging bag. Just think of a monk—a full-grown

monk—playing with children, bouncing a ball or playing marbles
fluttering the sleeves of his robe, torn and patched here and there,
with his begging bowl and staff thrown on the roadside! What a
funny and fantastic figure he must have cut in the eyes of the villagers! But Ryōkan was Ryōkan after all. He showed himself in
the best light while frolicking with youngsters.

One afternoon he was playing hide-and-seek and his turn to
hide came round; then he hid in a strawstack, taking it for granted that the children could never find him. After a while all the
children went home believing that Ryōkan had also left there.

The following morning at an early hour some farmers came
to the fields. How much surprised they were—to find Ryōkan
still carefully hiding himself in the haystack! What was more
shocking was that he put his finger across his lips and whispered,
"Hush, please don't speak so loudly! They will come and find
me." In a sense, he was more childlike than a child himself.

There are some people in the world who appear to be eccentric and even foolish yet somehow irresistibly appealing to the
depths of human heart. Here, in passing, we may as well say that
Ryōkan had turned out to be an eternal poet born out of the
autumnal glories covering Mt. Kugami and his poems were the
echoes sounding and resounding all over the skies glowing with
the evening sun under which stood the lofty figures of Mt.
Kugami and others. He sings in one of his poems as follows:

55. None are so foolhardy as I
     And yet I look on even plants and trees
     As my good neighbors. Indeed how awkward
     It is to make distinction between the awaken and not!

I laugh at my broken clay and go across a stream
Showing my knees bare.
When spring comes, I go forth into the village
Carrying a wallet with me.
So far I have only managed to get along!
Of course I am not escaping from the world
Though you may be tempted to think so.

頑愚信無比
草木以為隣
懶問迷悟歧
自笑老朽身
褒脛間渉水
携囊行歩春
聊可保此生
非敢厭世塵

Reading through these lines, you may be persuaded to believe
that he had a low opinion of himself; but this is not true.
Comparing himself with the natural world, he could not but feel
himself crooked and twisted and he wanted to be as natural and
full of life as nature herself. This philosophy of his he expressed in
his own way.

Cedar path.

The Poems

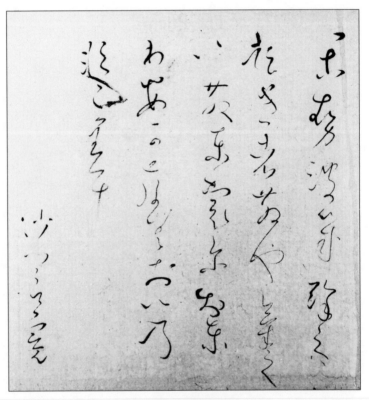

Ryōkan's calligraphy.

Tanka

SHORT POEMS

56. Once we start to bounce a ball,
    We will only be led on to,
    Counting: one, two, three, four, five, six, seven,
       eight, nine, ten,
    Only to start again—from the beginning!

    つきてみよ　ひふみよいむな　ここのとを
    　　とうと納めて　また始まるを
    Tsukite miyo　hifumi yoimuna　kokonoto o
    　　tōto osamete　mata hajimaru o

57. I strolled out to the village begging rice,
    But I found myself spending much time
    Picking up violets,
    Innocently smiling in the spring fields.

    飯乞ふと　わが来しかども　春の野に
    　　すみれ摘みつゝ　時を経にけり
    Ii kou to　waga koshika do mo　haru no no ni
    　　sumire tsumitsutsu　toki o heni keri

58. Gentle rains in spring, showers in summer,
    And a spell of fine weather in the fall.
    May the world glide on smoothly!
    May they bless me with sweet rice!

    春は雨　夏夕立ちに　秋旱り
    　　世の中よかれ　われ　飯乞はむ
    Haru wa ame　natsu yūdachi ni　aki hideri
    　　yononaka yokare　ware　ii kowamu

59. No more cloudy sky
    And now I will go a-begging
    Ready to receive
    Heaven's bounties to the full!

    雲出でし　空ははれけり　托鉢の
    　　こゝろのまゝに　天の与へを
    Kumo ideshi　sora wa hare keri　takuhatsu no
    　　kokoro no mama ni　ten no atae o

60. Tonight we have met
    But tomorrow you'll be gone—
    Beyond the mountain ridge far;
    Then again in my hut will I live alone!

    今宵会ひ　明日は山路を　へだてなば
    　　独りや住まむ　もとのいほりに
    Koyoi ai　asu wa yamaji o　hedate naba
    　　hitori ya sumamu　moto no ihori ni

61. Holding a bottle of sweet saké
    You urged me to drink;
    And how I went on drinking,
    Fascinated by the sweet wine!

    さすたけの　君がすゝむる　うま酒に
    　　我れ酔ひにけり　そのうま酒に
    Sasutake no　kimi ga susumuru　umazake ni
    　　ware yoi nikeri　sono umazake ni

62. Sleeping under the balmy skies
    Drinking, drinking to the full
    Dreaming of sweet flowers
    Lying under a cherry in bloom.

    ひさかたの　のどけき空に　酔ひ伏せば
    　　夢も妙なり　花の木の下
    Hisakata no　nodokeki sora ni　yoifuse ba
    　　yume mo taenari　hana no ki no shita

63. Maybe some rain is pattering;
    Maybe the trees in the ravine are whispering
    Or it may be the maple leaves scattering
    In a gale at midnight.

    ひさかたの　降りくる雨か　谷の音か
    　　夜は嵐に　散るもみじ葉か
    Hisakata no　furikuru ame ka　tani no ne ka
    　　yoru wa arashi ni　chiru momijiba ka

64. Would that I may come upon
    Someone of a like mind
    And have a talk with him
    In my hut all night through!

    世の中に　同じ心の人もがな
    　　草のいほりに　一夜語らむ
    Yononaka ni　onaji kokoro no hito mo gana
    　　kusa no ihori ni　hitoyo kataramu

65. How about taking a few cups of wine
    In my temporal abode
    Supported by the bamboo pillars
    Protected by the hanging straw blinds?

    わが宿は　竹の柱に　菰すだれ
    　　強ひて食しませ　ひと杯の酒
    Waga yado wa　take no hashira ni　komosudare
    　　shiite oshi mase　hitotsuki no saké

66. These are the wild parsleys
    I picked for you
    Going out into the fields
    During a lull in the rain.

    さすたけの　きみがみためと　ひさかたの
    　　雨間に出でて　摘みし芹ぞこれ
    Sasutake no　kimi ga mitame to　hisakata no
    　　amema ni idete　tsumishi seri zo kore

67. But for the sheer loneliness
    Of a mountain hut in winter,
    What could I treat you to
    As I can offer nothing else.

    山里の　冬の寂しさ　なかりせば
    　何をか君が　饗草にせむ

    Yamazato no　fuyu no sabishisa　nakari seba
    　nani oka kimi ga　aegusa ni semu

68. How it snows in February!
    Isn't this because
    Even the weather won't let you go
    You, who dropped in after a long absence?

    如月に　雪のひまなく　降ることは
    　たまたま来ます　君をやらじと

    Kisaragi ni　yuki no hima naku　furu kotowa
    　tamatama kimasu　kimi o yaraji to

69. Maples on this mountain
    Will shine no more!
    For when you are gone
    How can they?

    この山の　紅葉もけふは　限りかな
    　君し帰らば　色はあらまじ

    Kono yama no　momiji mo kyōwa　kagiri kana
    　kimi shi kaeraba　iro wa aramaji

70. Come again, come again,
    To my grassy hut
    Coming through the pampas grass
    Wet heavy with dew-drops!

    またも来よ　柴のいほりを　いとはずば
    　すゝき尾花の　露をわけわけ
    Matamo koyo　shiba no ihori o　itowazuba
    　susuki obana no　tsuyu o wakewake

71. If you won't mind
    The pines soughing
    And the storm-covered mountain,
    Come again tramping the shady path of cedars!

    谷の声　峰の嵐を　いとはずば
    　重ねてたどれ　杉のかげ道
    Tani no koe　mine no arashi o　itowazuba
    　kasanete tadore　sugi no kagemichi

72. I hold up in my hands
    The seven pink pomegranates
    Bowing low before them
    The gifts from the warmth within.

    紅の　七つのたからを　もろ手もて
    　おしいただきぬ　人のたまもの
    Kurenai no　nanatsu no takara o　morote mote
    　oshiitadakinu　hito no tamamono

73. How often I changed my place
    Looking for a better spot!
    But could I find a better one
    Than Mt. Kugami? No!

    いづこにも　替へ国すれど　わが心
    　　国上の里に　まさるとこなし
    Izuko nimo　kae kuni suredo　waga kokoro
    　　Kugami no sato ni　masarutoko nashi

74. If someone should ask me
    Where my hut stands
    My answer would be,
    "It stands east of the rim of the Milky Way."

    わが宿を　いづこと問わば　答ふべし
    　　天の川原の　はしの東と
    Waga yado o　izuko to towaba　kotaubeshi
    　　amano kawara no　hashi no higashi to

75. I have been wandering
    Like a floating cloud
    As I have no place to stay in;
    Thus I have lived so far.

    浮雲の　いづこを宿と　定めねば
    　　心のまにまに　日を送りつゝ
    Ukigumo no　izuku o yado to sadameneba
    　　kokoro no manimani　hi o okuri tsutsu

76. Of course I do not shun the world;
    I have just fallen into this groove
    And have lived on till now
    Yes, just this and nothing more.

    世の中を　厭ひはつとは　なけれども
    　　慣れしよすがに　日を送りつゝ
    Yono naka o   itoi hatsu to wa   nakere domo
    　　nareshi yosuga ni   hi o okuri tsutsu

77. I don't care for my body
    Weak and brittle as it is;
    But I would like to go on
    For as long as I'm allowed.

    なよ竹の　はしたなる身は　なほざりに
    　　いざ暮さまし　ひと日ひと日を
    Nayo take no   hashitanaru mi wa   naozari ni
    　　iza kurasamashi   hitohi hitohi o

78. Where, I wonder, is a cuckoo wandering?
    The cuckoo-bird I heard screaming
    At midnight
    As I was wending my way home.

    いづちへか　啼きて行くらむ　ほとゝぎす
    　　小夜ふけがたに　帰るさの道
    Izuchi e ka   nakite yukuramu   hototogisu
    　　sayofukegata ni   kaeru sa no michi

79. Wrapped in the evening fog
    Stands the village in the distance
    And I was going home alone
    Treading the cedar path.

   夕霧に　をちの里べは　埋もれぬ
   　　杉立つ宿に　帰るさの道

   Yūgiri ni   ochi no satobe wa   uzumorenu
   　　sugi tatsu yado ni   kaeru sa no michi

80. Among the trees and bushes
    Luxuriantly growing wild
    My hut stands buried,
    Where none would care to visit.

   わくらばに　訪ふ人もなき　わが宿は
   　　夏木立のみ　生ひ茂りつゝ

   Wakuraba ni   tou hito mo naki   waga yado wa
   　　natsu kodachi nomi   oi shigeri tsutsu

81. Ah, Cuckoo-bird,
    Don't cry so often!
    A homeless wanderer is lonely enough
    Even without your screaming.

   ほとゝぎす　いたくな啼きそ　さらでだに
   　　草の枕は　淋しきものを

   Hototogisu   itakuna naki so   saradedani
   　　kusano makura wa   sabishikimono o

82. Autumn has advanced so far
    And my forlornness has grown so deep.
    Let me confine myself in the grassy hut
    Pulling the blinds down tight.

    秋もやや　うらさびしくぞ　なりにける
    　　草のいほりを　いざ戸鎖してむ
    Aki mo yaya　urasabishikuzo　nari nikeru
    　　kusa no ihori o　iza tozashi temu

83. Oh, Night Wind,
    Stop thy wild blow
    As I live alone
    In my wood-log cabin!

    小夜嵐　いたくな吹きそ　さらでだに
    　　柴のいほりの　さびしきものを
    Sayo arashi　itaku na fukiso　saradedani
    　　shiba no ihori no　sabishiki mono o

84. At midnight
    I hear a deer belling on the peak
    And as I wake up,
    Loneliness cuts me to the quick.

    小夜ふけて　高嶺の鹿の　声きけば
    　　寝ざめさびしく　物やおもはる
    Sayo fukete　takane no shika no　koe kikeba
    　　nezame sabishiku　mono ya omowaru

85. If one asks
    What goes on inside this monk
    Pray answer as follows;
    "Nothing but what a passing wind whispers."

    この僧の　心を問はゞ　大空の
    　　風の便りに　つくと答へよ

    Kono sō no　kokoro o towaba　ōzora no
    　　kaze no tayori ni　tsuku to kotae yo

86. I am not escaping from the world;
    But what I like best is
    To enjoy myself alone
    Without mingling in the crowd.

    世の中に　まじらぬとには　あらねども
    　　ひとり遊びぞ　われはまされる

    Yononaka ni　majiranuto niwa　aranedomo
    　　hitori asobizo　ware wa masareru

87. I do not look upon myself
    As a poor, deserted monk.
    Why not look up?
    Doesn't the moon shine and flowers bloom?

    こと足らぬ　身とは思はじ　柴の戸に
    　　月もありけり　花もありけり

    Koto taranu　mi towa omowaji　shiba no to ni
    　　tsuki mo arikeri　hana mo arikeri

88. What can I compare
    The world to?
    Isn't it as empty
    As a dying echo?

世の中は　何に譬へむ　山彦の
　応ふる声の　むなしきがごと
*Yononaka wa　nani ni tatoemu　yamabiko no
　kotauru koe no　munashiki ga goto*

89. Why should you
    Argue on and on?
    Aren't phenomena nothing but
    The shadows of one cause?

かれこれと　何あげつらむ　世の中は
　一つの球の　影と知らずて
*Karekore to　nani agetsuramu　yononaka wa
　hitotsu no tama no　kage to shirazu te*

90. How helpless I have been
    Staying so long in my hut!
    My mind goes on wandering
    Like the seaweeds gathered.

草の庵に　立ちてみても　術ぞなき
　海人の刈る藻の　想いみだれて
*Kusa no ihori ni　tachi te mitemo　subezo naki
　ama no karumo no　omoi midare te*

91. I have been getting along
    Day after day in this way
    And I am quite at a loss
    How and where to live now.

    すべをなみ　一日二日と　過ぎぬれば
    　　今は我身の　おきどころなき
    Sube o nami   hitohi futahi to   suginureba
    　　ima wa wagami no   okidokoro naki

92. Why should I suffer
    From the worldly passions
    Had I not given up my life
    Even before I saw the light?

    うつしみの　うつゝ心の　やまぬかも
    　　生れぬ先に　わたしにし身を
    Utsushimi no   utsutsu gokoro no   yamanu kamo
    　　umarenu sakini   watashi nishi mi o

93. Hearing people speak
    About the troubles of the world
    I can't help but feel shocked
    As I am neither rock nor tree.

    うつせみの　人の憂けくを　聞けば憂し
    　　我れもさながら　岩木ならねば
    Utsusemi no   hito no nageku o   kikeba ushi
    　　waremo sanagara   iwaki nara neba

94. O that
    I were either a blade of grass or a tree
    Growing on a remote mountain
    Had I known the woebegone world!

    かくばかり　憂き世と知らば　奥山の
    　草にも木にも　ならましものを
    Kakubakari　ukiyo to shiraba　okuyama no
    　kusanimo kinimo　naramashi mono o

95. Birds sing here and there;
    Flowers smile on mountains all!
    And I feel spring coming strong on me!
    How can I contain myself?

    鳥は鳴く　四方の山べに　花は咲く
    　春の心の　置きどころなき
    Tori wa naku　yomo no yamabe ni　hana wa saku
    　haru no kokoro no　okidokoro naki

96. I have been idling away
    Day after day even in this world.
    How can I worry
    About the coming world?

    この世さへ　うからうからと　わたる身は
    　来ぬ世のことを　何思ふらむ
    Konoyo sae　ukara ukara to　wataru mi wa
    　konu yo no koto o　nani omou ramu

97. If my black robe is large enough
    How ready I would be
    To cover the whole sufferers
    With the robe I wear!

    墨染の　わが衣手の　ゆたならば
    　　まどしき民を　覆はましものを
    Sumi-zome no　waga koromode no　yutanaraba
    　madoshiki tami o　ōwa mashi mono o

98. I may lay down my clay
    Wherever I am destined to
    As I have given up my life
    For Buddha's mercy to lead me on

    いづこにも　朽ちやせなまし　み仏の
    　　み法のために　捨てしその身を
    Izuko nimo　kuchi ya senamashi　mihotoke no
    　minori no tame ni　suteshi sono mi o

99. Even in the remotest corner,
    Flowers will bloom
    If we attend them in earnest
    Nothing at all though we are.

    植えてみよ　花の育たぬ　里もなし
    　　心からこそ　身はいやしけれ
    Uete miyo　hana no sodatanu　sato mo nashi
    　kokoro kara koso　mi wa iyashi kere

100. In former days,
     I did just as my heart dictated me;
     But now, Heart,
     Obey me and do what I say.

     いにしへは　心のまゝに　従へど
     　今は心よ　我に従へ
     Inishie wa   kokoro no mama ni   shitagaedo
     　Ima wa kokoro yo   ware ni shitagae

101. Running water can be checked
     But what can't be called back
     Once it is gone
     Is time and tide already gone.

     ゆく水は　堰きとむことも　ありぬべし
     　返らぬものは　月日なりけり
     Yuku mizu wa   sekitomu koto mo   arinu beshi
     　kaeranu mono wa   tsukihi nari keri

102. In the garden here
     How triumphantly the plums
     Are blooming—and that
     When I have grown so old!

     この園の　梅の盛りと　なりにけり
     　わが老いらくの　時にあたりて
     Kono sono no   ume no sakari to   narinikeri
     　waga oiraku no   toki ni atarite

103. When I feel blue
And time hangs heavy,
I will go out to the fields
And pick mother's hearts.

もの思ひ　すべなき時は　うち出でて
　ふる野に生ふる　なずなをぞ摘む
Mono omoi　subenaki toki wa　uchi ide te
　furu no ni ouru　nazuna o zo tsumu

104. Don't you see
Things will change for good?
Both flowers early and late
Will vanish away sooner or later.

見ても知れ　いずれこの世は　常ならむ
　おくれ先だつ　花も残らず
Mite mo shire　izure konoyo wa　tsune naramu
　okure sakidatsu　hanamo nokorazu

105. I know
The world is not
How it appears to be;
And yet how evanescent things are!

ありてなき　世とは知るとも　空蝉の
　生きとしものは　死ぬるなりけり
Arite naki　yo towa shiru tomo　utsusemi no
　iki toshi mono wa　shinuru narikeri

106. In the world
     Things appearing to exist
     Will pass away one by one
     How long should I remain lamenting!

   あるはなく　亡きは数そふ　世の中に
     あはれ　いつまで　わが身　歎かむ
   Aru wa naku   naki wa kazu sou   yononaka ni
     aware   itsu made   waga mi   nagekamu

107. What can I rely upon
     When my pillar is broken?
     How can I depend on
     What has gone forever?

   亡きをりは　何をたよりに　思はまし
     有るにならひし　今日の心は
   Naki ori wa   nani o tayori ni   omowa mashi
     aruni naraishi   kyō no kokoro wa

108. I heard dead leaves
     Scattering away like showers
     And this morning I heard rain
     Pattering on my hut.

   はらはらと　降るは木の葉の　しぐれにて
     雨をけさ聞く　山里の庵
   Harahara to   furu wa konoha no   shigure nite
     ame o kesa kiku   yamazato no io

109. My hut stands on Mt. Kugami
   Buried under the thick snows
   Now I see snowflakes fluttering down
   Covering both the peaks and ridges.

   わが宿は　国上山もと冬ごもり
   　　峰にも尾にも　雪の降りつゝ
   Waga yado wa　Kugami yama moto fuyugomori
   　mine nimo o nimo　yuki no furitsutsu

110. When the moon shines
   Clean and clear
   Let me enjoy a plum-branch
   In the evening so quiet

   月影の　清き夕べに　梅の花
   　　おりてかざさむ　清きゆふべに
   Tsukikage no　kiyoki yūbe ni　ume no hana
   　orite kaza samu　kiyoki yūbe ni

111. I came to the village
   When the peaches were in bloom
   And there I saw a stream
   Changed into crimson!

   この里の　桃の盛りに　来て見れば
   　　流れにうつる　花のくれない
   Kono sato no　momo no sakari ni　kite mireba
   　nagare ni utsuru　hana no kurenai

112. O, that
   The spring evening would last for good
   When the fragrant cherry petals
   Are reeling up and down!

   かぐはしき　桜の花の　空に散る
   　　春の夕べは　暮れずもあらなむ
   Kaguwashiki　sakura no hana no　sora ni chiru
   　　haru no yūbe wa　kurezumo aranamu

113. Ah, autumn clovers
   Have covered the mountain path
   So thick that we can hardly find it
   As few people have come up there!

   たまぼこの　道まどふまで　秋萩は
   　　散りにけるかも　行く人なしに
   Tamaboko no　michi madou made　akihagi wa
   　　chiri nikeru kamo　yuku hito nashi ni

114. Heavy with dewdrops
   Some autumn flowers are blooming
   Though I have no one
   To present them to.

   白露に　みだれて咲ける　女郎花
   　　摘みておくらむ　その人なしに
   Shiratsuyu ni　midarete sakeru　ominaeshi
   　　tsumite okuramu　sono hito nashi ni

115. Hi, Grasshoppers,
Chirp your best this evening
As I have been longing
For your singing so patiently!

思ひつゝ　来つゝ聞きつる　この夕べ
　　声をつくして　鳴けきりぎりす
Omoi tsutsu　kitsutsu kiki tsuru　kono yūbe
　　koe o tsukushite　nake kirigirisu

116. Why shouldn't I go home
To my mountain hut
Treading along the cedar-path
Growing thick on Mt. Kugami?

国上山　杉の下道　ふみわけて
　　わが住む宿に　いざ帰りてむ
Kugamiyama　sugi no shita michi　fumi wakete
　　waga sumu yado ni　iza kaeri temu

117. In the world of dreams
I've been dreaming on and on
And upon waking up
How loneliness pierces me

夢の世に　また夢むすぶ　くさまくら
　　寝ざめさびしく　物思ふかな
Yume no yo ni　mata yume musubu　kusamakura
　　nezame sabishiku　mono omou kana

118. Where am I?
     Indeed where?
     But I hear no answer,
     Only a wind is soughing!

     わがこゝろ　有哉不有と　探り見れば
     　　空吹く風の　音ばかりなり
     Waga kokoro　ari ya naki ya to　saguri mireba
     　　sora fuku kaze no　oto bakari nari

119. I have nothing
     To look forward to
     So just let me be wafted on
     Like a cloud sailing high!

     浮雲の　待事も無き　身にしあれば
     　　風の心に　任すべらなり
     Ukigumo no　matsu koto mo naki　mi ni shi areba
     　　kaze no kokoro ni　makasubera nari

120. Pampas grasses and agueweeds
     Are waving in the autumn fields;
     But they might scatter away now
     As I have shown them to you.

     秋の野の　すゝき刈萱　ふじばかま
     　　君には見せつ　散らば散るとも
     Aki no no no　susuki karukaya　fujibakama
     　　kimi niwa misetsu　chiraba chiru tomo

121. How heartless white snowflakes are
     That they should be
     Piling thick on the ground
     On the very day when you are coming!

心なきもの　にもあるか　白雪は
　　君がくる日に　降るべきものか

Kokoro naki mono　nimo aruka　shirayuki wa
　　kimi ga kuru hi ni　furubeki mono ka

122. Dewdrops
     Are dancing on pampas grass.
     And how the moon is sailing
     Above them all!

秋風に　露はこぼれて　花すゝき
　　みだるゝ方に　月ぞいざよふ

Akikaze ni　tsuyu wa koborete　hanasusuki
　　midaruru kata ni　tsuki zo iza you

Poems Originally Written in Chinese

123. In this world, we meet only to part
     Like white clouds coming in and out of sight
     Leaving behind our faint traces,
     So faint that we can't trace them anywhere.

人　惟　來　相
間　留　去　逢
不ㇾ　霜　白　又
可ㇾ　毫　雲　相
尋　跡一　心　別

124. Going down into the basin
     To gather some orchids, I found
     The basin deep and dewy;
     And only when the evening twilight thickened,
     I came upon some. I was reminded of
     A friend of mine living far away

Separated by so many rivers and mountains.
And I can hardly tell if the blessed day will come
When we shall meet again.
Lifting up my neck, I look far up into the blue skies
Tears overflowing my eyes,
Trickling down like strings!

佇　引　良　山　悠　日　谷　下
立　領　晨　河　々　暮　邃　谷
涙　望　在　隔　懷　聊　霜　采
如　天　何　且　所　盈　露　崇
糸　末　時　長　思　把　滋　蘭

125. To the hedge cling
　　Two or three branches
　　With a few last mums
　　Lingering on it. And winter crows
　　Are on their wings,
　　Flying high above the woods and
　　Every peak is shining
　　In the evening glow.
　　Indeed this is the time
　　For a monk to go home
　　Tucking away the bowl.

籬　喬　千　正
外　林　峰　是
黃　蕭　万　收
花　疏　嶽　鉢
再　寒　只　僧
三　鴉　夕　歸
枝　飛　照　時

126. Whence did my life come?
　　　Whence does it go?
　　　I am sitting here alone under the window
　　　Calmly meditating all the while;
　　　But it doesn't reveal at all
　　　The origin of my life and much less
　　　Does it show the end thereof.
　　　It has simply been so so far
　　　And I know it will all end in nothing.
　　　So I will stay in the void for a while
　　　And how can I tell "good" from "evil"?
　　　I would rather stand above
　　　The triflings and live on calmly
　　　As long as I'm allowed!

我生何處來
去而何處之
獨坐蓬窗下
兀兀靜尋思
尋思不知始
焉能知其終
現在亦復然
展轉總是空
空中且與我
況有是與非
不如容些子
隨緣旦從容

127. None are so foolhardy as I
And so I look on plants and trees
As my good neighbors. Indeed how awkward
It is to make distinction between the awakened and not!
I laugh at my broken clay and go across a stream
Showing my knees bare.
When spring comes I go forth into the village
Carrying a wallet with me.
So far I have only managed to get along!
Of course I am not escaping from the world
Though you may be tempted to think so.

頑愚信無比
草木以為隣
懶問迷悟岐
自笑老朽身
褰脛間涉水
携囊行步春
聊可保此生
非敢厭世塵

128. Since I lived here,
     So far away from the maddening crowd
     I know not how many winters and springs
     Have gone. During all these years
     I have been feeding myself on the herbs of the fields
     And the rice my neighbors have spared.
     Heartily contented with the life
     Among the woods on the mountains
     Ready to enjoy eating under the trees,
     I am making the best and most
     Of my daily living. Especially
     When I come home, I may sit up or lie down
     As I am inclined to.
     What a blessing
     This life of mine has been to me!

幽樓地從占
不知幾冬春
菜只藜藿是
米自乞比隣
偏喜人事少
末厭林下貧
還來殊疏慵
坐臥任屈伸

129. Once in a while
     I just let time wear on
     Leaning against a solitary pine
     Standing speechless,
     As does the whole universe!
     Ah, who can share
     This solitude with me?

與 茫 偶 獨
レ
誰 々 爾 倚
        二
共 滿 復 孤
同 天 移 松
歸 下 時 立
              一

130. Day after day
     I enjoy myself
     Playing with village children,
     Carrying two or three balls
     In my sleeve-pockets.
     I am good for nothing
     But how fully satisfied I am
     With this peaceful spring!

日々日々又日々
間伴二兒童一送二此身一
袖裏毬子両三箇
無能飽醉太平春

131. Now and then
I hear leaves falling
While sitting alone.
I have cut off my ties
With the world, and yet
Why should I shed tears?

坐時聞二落葉一
靜住是二出家一
從來斷二思量一
不レ覺涙沾レ巾

132. A long drawn winter night!
     Indeed how long it can last!
     The light is gone and no fire
     Flickers in the hearth.
     I only hear a night rain
     Drizzling, drizzling outside!

只	燈	冬	冬
聞	無	夜	夜
枕	焰	悠	長
上	兮	々	兮
夜	爐	何	冬
雨	無	時	夜
聲	炭	明	長

133. We should not be tempted by outward things,
     Keeping taciturn as much as possible;
     We should not take any food except when hungry
     And let our teeth meet only after we have awaked from
       a dream.
     Now I came to learn a little how to keep me in good
       health

Through reading *Hakuyu's Life.**
Truly when we are overflowing with the Cosmic Life,
We shall prove ourselves adamantine to evils!

紛々莫逐物
默々宜守口
飯喫腸飢始
齒叩夢覺後
我讀白幽傳
聊得養生趣
令氣常盈內
外邪何讒受

134. Thinking of the past,
　　　It has already gone;
　　　Thinking of the present,
　　　It is going too.
　　　We can't leave our footprints
　　　On the sands of time
　　　Since Time is passing on
　　　Sweeping away everything.
　　　Then how can we
　　　Make distinction
　　　Between a wise man and a fool?

---

* Hakuyū was a hermit who lived among the hills, kyoto in the middle of the Tokugawa period (1603–1867)

So I will live on
So long as my star shines
Waiting for it to sink.
Indeed, twenty years have gone
Since I perched on this mountain!

問古々己過
思今々亦然
展轉無蹤跡
誰愚又誰賢
隨緣消時月
保己待終焉
飄我來此地
回首二十年

135. Without a craving
I crave nothing
With a craving
I crave everything.
Among the mountains
I can feed myself on herbs
And get along
Wearing only one robe.
Rambling alone
I make friends
With deer and others.
I can join the village children
Singing loudly with them.

To wash my soiled ears clean,
I go to the stream
Under the rocks
And on the peaks I make friends
With the pines standing there.

無欲一切足
有求万事窮
淡菜可療饑
衲衣聊纏窮
獨往伴麋鹿
高歌和村童
洗耳岩下水
可意嶺上松

136. Everything turns out false;
　　　Everything turns out true
　　　According to your way of thinking.
　　　Falsehood does not exist outside truth
　　　Nor truth lies outside falsehood.
　　　Fellow truth-seekers,
　　　Why do you seek after truth only?
　　　I'd rather ask you if your mind
　　　To seek after truth is true or false.

是　試　只　如　妄　真　道　道
妄　要　管　何　外　外　真　妄
乎　覓　欲　修　別　更　一　一
是　底　覓　道　無　無　切　切
真　心　真　子　真　妄　真　妄

137. I feel the chilly touch in the autumn air
　　　And leaning on my staff,
　　　I feel the rising wind cold.
　　　A village in the distance is wrapped in the evening fog
　　　And a solitary shadow of a man is seen
　　　Going across the bridge in the fields!
　　　Some old crows are flying straight to their old nests,
　　　And some wild geese are seen flying across the skies
　　　In a bow-like formation.
　　　It is on such an evening
　　　That you might come upon a dark-robed monk
　　　Standing still—gazing into the flowing river.

立　唯　斜　老　行　孤　倚　秋
盡　有　雁　鴉　人　村　杖　氣
暮　緇　沒　宿　野　苦　風　何
江　衣　遙　故　橋　霧　稍　蕭
前　僧　天　林　邊　裏　寒　索

138. All mountains are buried under the frozen snow
     And on paths no living creatures are seen!
     Day in day out I sit facing the wall
     Though often snowdrifts blow in at the openings.

千峰凍雪合
万徑人跡絕
每日只面壁
時間灑窗雪

139. Across the frozen skies of winter
     Are flying the wild geese
     And all over the vacant mountain
     Dead leaves are flying up and down.
     I am treading back the foggy path alone
     Carrying an empty bowl.

青天寒雁鳴
空山木葉飛
日暮煙邨路
獨揭空盂歸

140. No path leads us to our spiritual awakening
    Nor do we find our destination.
    When we catch sight of
    Some state of enlightenment and pursue it directly
    We shall find it receding from us farther than ever.
    When we are going astray and yet trying to be spiritually
        awakened
    We shall run wide of the mark all the more!
    When we try to attain truth through theoretical
        investigation
    Or even when we feel we have found the Golden Mean,
    We may be treading the wrong road!
    Too much for me it is to impart to the others
    This subtle state of mind
    Accompanying this spiritual awakening of mine—
    Since when it is expressed, it will be torn into pieces!

大道元來沒程途
不知何處是本期
認境趁境々々愈遠
迷心覺心々々却非
仮說空有誘諸子
從契中道終墮歧
我這些子妙不傳
裁掛齒牙為支離

141. The whole world is as dishevelled as
    Torn up hemp-threads. As it has been
    In the past so will it be in the future and
    We shall be tired out while hovering about
    Here and there without attaining the true awakening.
    Though we may learn Buddha's Way
    So long as captured by the phenomenal,
    How can we realize the First Cause?
    But once we enter the Way of Zen and
    Abide by the Zen Principle then
    We can stand above the ever-changing world
    How can we be tempted to go otherwise?
    But once we go into the floating world
    We find ourselves pitilessly bewildered
    As so deftly expressed in the *Dōsan-roku.*

三界冗々事如麻
非適今兮自古然
渾為一句不了却
百年無端疲往還
經數名相不永邊
禪執寂靜竟難遷
因憶洞山好言語
出門即是草漫々

---

* The author of the *Dōsan-roku* was Dōsan (807–69) a great Chinese abbot who originated the Sōdō Sect of Zen.

142. No more wind;
No more flowers;
Birds scream once in a while
Deepening the silence all the more!
Should I still remain
Ignorant of Buddha's Benevolence?
Fie upon me!

風定花猶落
鳥啼山更幽
觀音妙知力

143. The ball of colored threads
I am hiding in my sleeves
Is more than 1,000 dollars worth!
In ball-bouncing, none can beat me.
Should someone ask me to tell him
The secret of ball-bouncing,
I'd only call out "One, two, three, four, five, six, and seven
That's all!"

袖裏繡毬值千金
謂言好手無等匹
箇中意旨若相問
一二三四五六七

144. Of an evening among the mountains
     When I sit with eyes closed,
     Worldly troubles will fade away.
     Leaning lightly on the straw stool
     I am facing the vacant window.
     I burn some incense, but
     It ceases to burn as the long night wears on.
     Hoarfrost lies thick on the ground
     But I have only a summer robe to wear
     Going out into the yard I see the moon
     Hanging far above the highest peak!

月　定　衣　香　寥　寂　人　冥
上　起　單　消　々　々　間　目
最　庭　白　玄　對　倚　万　千
高　際　露　夜　虚　蒲　慮　嶂
峰　步　濃　永　窻　團　空　夕

145. I had been up on the mountain
    To gather firewood and when I came back
    The sun had already leaned west.
    Someone had brought some damson-plums and potatoes
    And left them under the window.
    The plums were wrapped in a paper bag
    And the potatoes, in green grass; beside them
    Was a piece of paper with the sender's name.
    The food is always lacking
    Among the mountains
    And the turnips are the only vegetables I can find.
    Thanking from the bottom of my heart, I did it
    With bean-paste and salt. As I would often feel hungry
    I ate three bowls and felt satisfied. Had my poet-friend
    Brought me a bottle of wine, how nice it would have
        been!
    Twenty percent of what I was given,
    I put away in the kitchen; then
    I went out for a walk patting my full belly,
    Wondering what I should do with the rest.

In six days from now
The anniversary of Buddha's awakening
Will come round
And I have been wondering
What I should offer to Buddha.
The prices of commodities
Have zoomed up tremendously
And my whole property wouldn't buy
Things—even a mere basketful.
Fortunately I was given this much
So I will offer them to Buddha;
The damson-plums as dessert and
Potatoes as soup.

上山采束薪
歸來日已傾
誰以李與芋
投之窗下棚
李盛袋芋青蔞
別有一紙題姓名
山中連日無兼味
偶得菜根只蔓菁
急著釜底下塩豉
饑腸灑來稍如飽
三飡喫了再經會
惟恨詩人不携罍
余留二分藏厨下
捫腹逍遙再成道
却後六日成丹誠
不知何以表丹誠
渠儂隣寺常乏物
多求市城又十倍
市城歲資不盈籃
傾盡家晚不盈籃
今年幸以故老生
供養西天古如何
借問供養其如何
李充茶菓芋是羹

Ryōkan as a Human Being

About thirty years have passed since Mr. Hikosaku Yanagishima, professor at Doshisha University, and I published the book Ryōkan the Great Fool *in April, 1969 (Kyoto Seika Junior College Press, Kyoto, Japan).*

During these past thirty years, I have encountered the death of this honored professor, Mr. Yanagishima, who passed away without knowing that Ryōkan's fame is spreading all over the world. It was our privilege and life work to study and write about this Great Ryōkan since he had enchanted both of us throughout our lives.

This time I am writing again of this Great Monk, Ryōkan, being led by the mysterious "spirit and hand," to add one chapter entitled "Ryōkan as a Human Being" to our original edition.

In 1779 at the age 22, Ryōkan left home to become a monk. There are many reasons given for his having done so, but they all stem from supposition. The true facts are unknown. According to his Zen master, Kokusen, a monk at Entsūji, soon thereafter he entered Tamashima Temple in Bitchū Province, now called Okayama Prefecture. When he was 26 years old, his mother died. At 33 he was given authorization to become a monk by his master, Kokusen, and at 38, his father died. It is said that at this time he tried to commit suicide by drowning himself in the Katsura River in Kyoto. However, it seems that this same year, he returned to his birthplace near Izumozaki, and by the time he was 47, he apparently had already moved to and been living on Mount Kugami. Be that as it may, for the ten years from the time he left the temple in Bitchū until he was settled on Mount Kugami, very little is known about his true whereabouts and doings. It is thought that he was what is called a wandering monk. In spite of this uncertainty, in order to discuss the man Ryōkan, it is said that this period was a very important time in his life. For this reason, there are two or three well-known accounts that I would like to share with you now.

MK

* * *

My name is Banjo. When I was still a youth, traveling through the province of Tosa, and was about seven miles from the castle town, not only did the rain come pounding down, but it began to become dark as well. A short distance from the main road I saw a small, ramshackle hut at the foot of a mountain. Thinking I might be able to spend the night there, I went only to find a skinny, pale-faced monk sitting alone by the hearth who told me that he had no food to offer me nor had he any bedding to protect me from the wind. "I don't need anything so long as I can get out of the rain," I said and without waiting for a reply, took off my shoes and made myself at home.

Until late at night we sat across from each other at the open hearth, but after our first remarks, the monk said not another word. Furthermore, he didn't sit in meditation, nor did he sleep, nor even pray to Amitabha, and no matter what I said to him, he would only smile. I thought in my heart of hearts that this man must be a loony!

That night I slept by the hearth and when I awoke at break of day the next morning, the monk lay fast asleep, using his arm as a pillow. It was still raining, but even harder than the day before, making it impossible to start out. I asked him if I could stay at least until it let up a little, to which he replied that I might stay as long as I liked. With this answer, I was even happier than the night before. That morning for breakfast he served me a gruel of barley flour dissolved in hot water.

Looking around the hut, I saw one wooden Buddha and a small table near the window. Two books lay on the table. Other than these things, there was nothing else in the hut. I opened the books to see what they were and found them to be Chinese volumes of the Chuang-tzu. Classic poetry written in cursive style, apparently by the monk, had been placed between the pages.

Since I had never studied Chinese poetry, I could not tell whether these poems were well-written or not, but the calligraphy was indeed splendid. For that reason, I took two folding fans and a calligraphy brush from my bag and begged him to please write something on them for me which he did immediately. One was a picture of a nightingale on the branch of a plum tree and the other was a picture of Mt. Fuji. Beneath the picture of Mt. Fuji I remember that he wrote "Who wrote this? Ryōkan of Echigo."

The rain had not let up by nightfall, so just like the day before, the monk and I slept on either side of the open hearth. By the next morning, however, the rain had completely stopped, and the sunshine was sparkling. After eating the usual barley gruel for breakfast, I took out my money and offered to pay for the two nights I had stayed there, but the way he said "No, thank you" convinced me that no amount of coaxing would sway him to accept. Knowing that insisting on his taking some monetary gift would be rude, I offered instead to give him some paper and cards for writing poems. These he received with delight.

This all happened over thirty years ago, but recently in the book, *Hokuetsu Kidan* (Interesting Tales from Northern Echigo) by Tachibana Mochiyo, I found this written. "Ryōkan of Echigo—I've forgotten the name of the place—was the eldest son of a well-known family there. From childhood he loved reading, but his calligraphy, especially, was superlative. Because he wanted to follow the classic masters, body and soul, even living like them, he left his wealthy home, giving up his inheritance. His whereabouts became unknown." After reading about the extraordinary life this man led in his shabby hut, I felt that certainly the monk I met in Tosa must have been the one and the same man. Deeply moved, I sobbed quietly all night thinking about the time I spent with him.

All this happened over twenty years ago, but I have collected and written down all that I saw and heard at that time, calling this small tome of reminisces, *Nezame no Tomo* (A Bedside Companion). Recently, after reading it, the abbot of Denchu-an said to me that because he also was born in Echigo and misses Ryōkan, he would really appreciate a copy. Not wanting to refuse, I have herewith written it down.

Recorded in early summer, the second year of Kōka (1845)
Banjo, 70 years old, owner of the Camellia Garden

* * *

Near the seaside at a place called Gōmoto, there was an unused
hut. One evening a wandering monk came to inquire if he might
live in it. The next day he went to the neighboring village in
order to beg for food, returning [to the hut] whenever he had collected enough to eat. If he had food to spare, he shared it with
beggars, birds, and animals. In this way six months passed. The
people were attracted by his superlative character, and impressed
with his love of virtue, giving him clothing which he received
thankfully and shared with others who also were in need. The
place where he lived was a mere seven miles or so from his birthplace, Izumozaki. For this reason, the people who lived nearby
told my brother that this monk was certainly the son of the house
of Tachibana. My brother went immediately to the seaside hut
near Gōmoto, but no one was there though the dilapidated door
was easily opened. On entering, he found a low table upon which
there were an ink stone and writing brush, an open hearth, and
one earthenware pot. The crumbling walls were covered with
poems. Reading them, my brother felt separated from this world
and attracted to the spiritual world of Zen; it was as if his heart
and mind had become as clear as the moon. When he returned,
my brother told his neighbors that the calligraphy was without
doubt that of Ryōkan. They lost no time telling all this to
Ryōkan's family. Some of his relatives then came to take him
home, but he declined their proposal. Moreover, even though
they sent him food and clothing, he returned all that was not nec-
essary. Soon thereafter his whereabouts became unknown.

* * *

Later in his life, there was another episode with a disciple named Teishin, a nun. He met this beautiful nun at the age of 69 when Teishin was 29. They had exchanged the poems that were full of humanity and sometimes even humorous. Their relationship was very spiritual and deep. After his death, this nun devoted her life to compile Ryōkan's poems and writings left with his friends and acquaintances and published a book named *Hachisu no Tsuyu* (A Dewdrop from a Lotus). This book contributes a great deal to our learning of Ryōkan. It is my honor to introduce these poems in this chapter.

* * *

Correspondence between Ryōkan and Teishin

On my first visit to Ryōkan
1. Wondering if it's a dream,
   I'm filled with joy,
   Never awake me, if it's a dream.
   Leave me, please, in this joy, forever.
   —Teishin

（はじめてあひ見奉りて）
きみにかく　あひ見ることの　うれしさも
　　まださめやらぬ　ゆめかとぞおもふ　（貞心）
Kimi ni kaku　aimiru koto no　ureshisamo
　　mada sameyaranu　yume katozo omou

(Answer)

2. Slumbering in the dream land,
   Talking about the dream.
   Why not float our dream
   On the stream of eternity.

   —Ryōkan

（御かへし）

ゆめのよに　かつまどろみて　ゆめをまた
　　かたるもゆめも　それがまにまに　（良寛）

Yume no yo ni   katsu madoromite   yume o mata
　　kataru mo yume mo   sore ga mani mani

It became late as we talked on so many serious subjects such as religion, poems, morals, etc.

3. Chilly, so chilly,
   Night has deepened,
   Look,
   The moon is high up in the sky.

   —Ryōkan

（いとねもごるなる道のものがたりに夜もふけぬれば）

しろたへの　ころもでさむし　あきのよの
　　つきなかぞらに　すみわたるかも　（良寛）

Shirotae no   koromode samushi   aki no yo no
　　tsuki nakazora ni   sumiwataru kamo

And still I want to talk on with him

4. Long long years,
   Yes, endlessly long years,
   Being together face to face,
   Never asking the moon the time to go.

   —Teishin

（されどなほあかぬここちして）
むかひゐて　ちよもやちよも　見てしがな
　　そらゆくつきの　こととはずとも　（貞心）

Mukai ite　chiyo mo yachiyo mo　miteshigana
　　sora yuku tsuki no　koto towazu tomo

(Answer)

5. If our hearts are unchanged,
   Like vines growing on a tree.
   Let's be together,
   For all eternity.

   —Ryōkan

（御かへし）
こころだに　かはらざりせば　はふつたの
　　たえずむかはむ　千よもやちよも　（良寛）

Kokoro dani　kawarazariseba　hau tsuta no
　　taezu mukawan　chiyo mo yachiyo mo

Now I have to go

6. Good-bye, dear Master,
   Please let me come again,

Tracing along the path,
Through weeds growing so thick.

—Teishin

（いざかへりなんとて）
たちかへり　またもとひこむ　たまぼこの
　　みちのしばくさ　たどりたどりに　（貞心）

Tachikaeri　matamo toikomu　tamaboko no
　　michi no shiba kusa　tadori tadori ni

(Answer)

7. Please come again, please,
   If you don't mind the poor hut.
   Why not come and see me again,
   Through the dewy way of eulalia.

—Ryōkan

（御かへし）
またもこよ　しばのいほりを　いとはずば
　　すすきをばなの　つゆをわけわけ　（良寛）

Matamo koyo　shiba no iori o　itowazu ba
　　susuki obana no　tsuyu o wake wake

After a while, I received a letter from him

8. Have you forgotten?
   Or is the way lost?
   I keep waiting and waiting.
   In vain, in pain.

—Ryōkan

(ほどへてみせうそこ給はりけるなかに)
きみやわする　みちやかくるる　このごろは
　　まてどくらせど　おとづれのなき　（良寛）

Kimi ya wasuru　michi ya kakururu　kono goro wa
　　matedo kurasedo　otozure no naki

(My answer to him)
9. Disturbed
By rootless rumor,
I am imprisoned
Against the desire of my heart.
　　　　　　　　—Teishin

(御かへし奉るとて)
ことしげき　むぐらのいほに　とぢられて
　　みをばこころに　まかせざりけり　（貞心）

Koto shigeki　mugura no iho ni　tojirarete
　　mi oba kokoro ni　makase zari keri

10. The moon above the mountain
Casts its light all around,
And yet,
Thin clouds are still floating over the peaks.
　　　　　　　　—Teishin

やまのはの　つきはさやかに　てらせども
　　まだはれやらぬ　みねのうすぐも　（貞心）

Yama no ha no　tsuki wa sayaka ni　terase domo
　　mada hare yaranu　mine no usugumo

11. So pure is the light of the moon,
    It shines out all of the earth,
    As far as from Kara[1]
    To Yamato.[2]

    —Ryōkan

ひさかたの　つきのひかりの　きよければ
　　てらしぬきけり　からもやまとも　（良寛）

Hisakata no tsuki no hikari no kiyokereba
　　terashi nuki keri karamo yamatomo

* * *

Ryokan's Instruction to Teishin

Falsehood and truth, darkness and light, will become clear
when the thin clouds over the peaks disappear. It's the
eternal law. Do you agree?

むかしもいまも　うそもまことも　やみもひかりも
はれやらぬ　みねのうすぐも　たちさりて
のちのひかりと　おもはずやきみ

Mukashimo imamo usomo makotomo
yamimo hikarimo hareyaranu
mine no usugumo tachisari te
nochi no hikari to omowazuya kimi

---

[1] Kara: old name for China
[2] Yamato: old name for Japan

Never cheat though others might.
Never quarrel though others might.
You can always keep your mind peaceful
Only by chasing away those worldly thoughts.

ひとはいつはるとも　いつはらじ
人はあらそうとも　あらそわじ
いつわり　あらそい　すててこそ
つねにこころは　のどかなれ

Hito wa itsuwaru tomo   itsuwaraji
hito wa arasou tomo   arasowaji
itsuwari   arasoi   sutetekoso
tsune ni kokoro wa
nodoka nare

In early spring, I sent him a letter

12. Darkness as well as light has gone,
    Only the bright moon
    At dawn!

　　　　　　　　　　—Teishin

（はるのはじめつかたせうそこたてまつるとて）
さめぬれば　やみもひかりも　なかりけり
　　ゆめじをてらす　ありあけのつき　（貞心）

Same nureba   yami mo hikari mo   nakari keri
*   yumeji o terasu   ariake no tsuki*

13. How serene the moonlight is!

It embraces us all,
Even falsehood and truth,
All, all, equally.

—Teishin

われもひとも　うそもまことも　へだてなく
　てらしぬきける　つきのさやけさ　（貞心）

Ware mo hito mo　uso mo makoto mo　hedate naku
　terashi nuki keru　tsuki no sayakesa

(Answer)

14. What shall I compare
Your precious letter in early spring to?
All the jewels and gold
Lose their color.

—Ryōkan

（御かへし）

あめがしたに　みつるたまより　こがねより
　はるのはじめの　きみがおとづれ　（良寛）

Ame ga shita ni　mitsuru tama yori　kogane yori
　haru no hajime no　kimi ga otozure

15. Never forget the pledge
We made before Buddha,
Though we may live
In the afterworld to come.

—Ryōkan

りょうせむの　しゃかのみまへに　ちぎりてし
　　ことなわすれそ　世はへだつとも　（良寛）

Ryōsemu no   shaka no mimae ni   chigiri teshi
　　koto na wasureso   yo wa hedatsu tomo

(Answer)

16. I swear never to forget the promise
　　We made before Buddha,
　　Though we may live
　　In the world to come.

　　　　　　　　　—Teishin

（御かへし）

りょうせむの　しゃかのみまへに　ちぎりてし
　　ことはわすれじ　よはへだつとも　（貞心）

Ryōsemu no   shaka no mimae ni   chigiri teshi
　　koto wa wasureji   yo wa hedatsu tomo

On leaving the hut

17. Good-bye, dear teacher;
　　I wish you well,
　　Till we meet again.
　　Among the merrily singing cuckoos.

　　　　　　　　　—Teishin

（御いとま申すとて）

いざさらば　さきくてませよ　ほととぎす
　　しばなくころは　またも来てみん　（貞心）

Iza saraba   sakikute maseyo   hototogisu
  shibanaku koro wa   mata mo kitemin

18. This floating cloud,
    Where shall it wait for you,
    When all the mountain
    Fills with the sweet melody of cuckoos?
    —Ryōkan

うきぐもの　みにしありせば　ほととぎす
　しばなくころは　いづこにまたむ　（良寛）

Ukigumo no   minishi ariseba   hototogisu
  shibanaku koro wa   izuko ni matamu

But soon I visited him
19. Again I've come,
    Impatient to see you,
    Finding the narrow path
    Thickly covered with summer grass.
    —Teishin

（されどそのほどをまたず又とひ奉りて）
あきはぎの　はなさくころを　まちとをみ
　なつぐさわけて　またも　きにけり　（貞心）

Akihagi no   hana saku koro o   machitoomi
  natsugusa wakete   mata mo   kinikeri

(Answer)

20. Impatiently waiting for the *hagi*[3] to bloom
    And you to come
    Through the dewy grass so thickly grown,
    Now you're here!

    —Ryōkan

（御かへし）
あきはぎの　さくをとを見と　なつぐさの
　　つゆをわけわけ　とひしきみはも　（良寛）

Akihagi no   saku o toomi to   natsugusa no
　　tsuyu o wake wake   toishi kimi wamo

One summer day, I visited him but he was out. The scent of a lotus sweetly filled the vacant hut.

21. There was none
    But a lotus,
    Filling the hut with its scent.
    How precious it was!

    —Teishin

きてみれば　ひとこそみえね　いほもりて
　　にほふはちすの　はなのとふとさ　（貞心）

Kite mireba   hito koso mie ne   io morite
　　niou hachisu no   hana no tōtosa

---

[3]*hagi:* Japanese bush clover

(Answer)
22. Nothing can I offer you,
But a sweet smelling lotus
Blooming with all its heart
Only to welcome you.

　　　　　　　—Ryōkan

（御かへし）
みあへする　ものこそなけれ　をがめなる
　　はちすのはなを　みつつしのばせ　（良寛）
Miae suru　mono koso nakere　ogamenaru
　　hachisu no hana o　mitsutsu shinobase

Once I said to him, "Your complexion is dark, and also your robe is black, so I may call you a crow from now on?" He said, "Wonderful. It's much to the point."

23. Where shall I fly off to
From tomorrow?
Now that they call me a crow
I'm destined to go on a journey.

　　　　　　　—Ryōkan

いづこへも　たちてをゆかむ　あすよりは
　　からすてふ名を　ひとのつくれば　（良寛）
Izuko emo　tachiteo yukamu　asu yori wa
　　karasu chō na o　hito no tsukureba

24. Since the mountain crow flies to the village
    Please take a young crow with him, too.
    Weak as its wings are
    It will surely follow him.

    —Teishin

やまがらす　さとにいゆかば　子がらすも
　　いざなひてゆけ　はねよわくとも　（貞心）

Yamagarasu　sato ni iyukaba　ko garasu mo
　　izanaite yuke　hane yowaku tomo

(Answer)

25. I don't mind taking it, though
    They may whisper to each other,
    Saying, "They are a couple"
    What shall we do?

    —Ryōkan

（御かへし）
いざなひて　ゆかばゆかめど　ひとのみて
　　あやし見らば　いかにしてまし　（良寛）

Izanaite　yukaba yukamedo　hito no mite
　　ayashi miraba　ika ni shite mashi

(Answer)

26. A kite is a kite,
    A sparrow is a sparrow,

A heron is a heron,
A crow and a crow, what's wrong?
—Teishin

（御かへし）
とびはとび　すずめはすずめ　さぎはさぎ
　　からすとからす　なにがあやしき　（貞心）
Tobi wa tobi　suzume wa suzume　sagi wa sagi
　　karasu to karasu　nani ga ayashiki

Through these poems, we can see that Ryōkan is teaching Teishin with humorous poetry and Teishin answers it splendidly.

It became dark and he left saying that he would visit the next morning.

27. Now I'll go,
Sleep here peacefully.
I'm sure to come back
Early tomorrow morning.
—Ryōkan

いざさらば　われはかえらむ　きみはここに
　　いやすくいねよ　はやあすにせむ　（良寛）
Iza saraba　ware wa kaeramu　kimi wa koko ni
　　iyasuku ineyo　haya asu ni semu

Next day, he came to see me early in the morning.

28. Writing poems or playing with balls,
    Walking through the fields,
    All seems to be fun.
    Let's do whatever you like.
    　　　　　　　　　—Teishin

　　うたやよまむ　てまりやつかん　野にやでむ
　　　きみがまにまに　なしてあそばむ　（貞心）
    Uta ya yomamu   temari ya tsukan   no niya demu
    　kimi ga mani mani   nashite asobamu

29. Writing poems or playing with balls,
    Walking through the fields,
    All seems to be fun.
    But hard to choose one.
    　　　　　　　　　—Ryōkan

　　うたやよまむ　てまりやつかむ　野にやでむ
　　　こころひとつを　さだめかねつも　（良寛）
    Uta ya yomamu   temari ya tsukamu   no niya demu
    　kokoro hitotsu o   sadame kanetsumo

*At the end of December, I heard he was seriously ill. I hastened
to see him.*

30. When? When?
    How eagerly I've been waiting.

Now that you are here
What more do I want?

—Ryōkan

いついつと　まちにしひとは　きたりけり
いまはあひ見て　なにかおもはむ　（良寛）

Itsu itsu to　machinishi hito wa　kitari keri
　imawa aimite　nanika omowamu

Since then, I've been at his bedside, attending on him night and day. He was getting weaker and weaker.

31. I'll not stop eating all at once,
    But wait for the time to go.
    Eating less and less
    Till my time will come.

—Ryōkan

うちつけに　飯絶つとには　あらねども
　かつ安らひて　時をしまたむ　（良寛）

Uchitsuke ni　ii tatsu to niwa　arane domo
　katsu yasuraite　toki o shimatamu

32. We are destined to live
    Beyond life and death.
    Yet, alas!
    How can I bear this destiny!

—Teishin

いきしにの　さかひはなれて　すむみにも
　　さらぬわかれの　あるぞかなしき （貞心）

Ikishini no   sakai hanarete   sumu mi nimo
　saranu wakare no   aru zo kanashiki

(Answer)

33. Showing its front and back
    A falling maple leaf.

                              —Ryōkan

（御かへし）
うらをみせ　おもてをみせて
　　ちるもみぢ （良寛）

Ura o mise   omote o misete
　chiru momiji

This short poem was not one of his, but from time to time, he quoted it.

* * *

What shall I leave as my memento?
Flowers in spring,
Mountain cuckoos,
Scarlet leaves in autumn.

                              —Ryōkan

かたみとて　なにかのこさむ　春は花
山ほととぎす　はもみぢ葉　（良寛）

Katami tote   nani ka nokosamu   haru wa hana
yama hotogisu   aki wa momijiba

* * *

The Brief History of Teishin-ni* 1798–1872

A daughter of samurai, married to a doctor, who died a few years after marriage. Became a nun. In 1826, visited Ryōkan and was granted permission to be his disciple, learning the art of Tanka poetry. After Ryōkan's death, published his poems and writings. Died at 74 years of age, the same age as Ryōkan died.

---

ni: nun

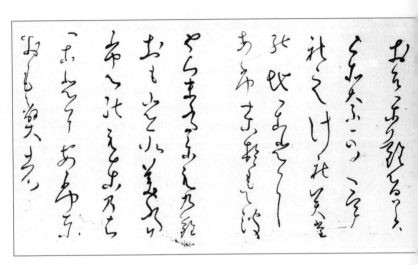

Ryōkan's calligraphy.

My Favorite Poems

Evidently Ryōkan was a man who had sacrificed everything to get in touch with the true meaning of life. He was a man who had grasped a most profound *satori* without knowing he had. Am I going too far if I say that in the Bible, too, we find some passages that Ryōkan would have shed tears of gratitude had he ever read them himself?

Truth beams on forever and such a life as Ryōkan lived will guide us as a beacon light that shines upon our way to follow—even in the succeeding pitch dark nights of our life.

1. Alas!
   Had I known this world so merciless
   Would I have grown trees or grass
   In the deep deep mountains.

   かくばかり　憂き世と知らば　奥山の
   草にも木にも　ならましものを
   *Kaku bakari   ukiyo to shiraba   okuyama no
   kusa nimo ki nimo   naramashi mono o*

2. If I'm asked
   What's this abandoned clay,
   My answer will be
      "Rain or wind as it likes."

   捨てし身を　いかにと問はば　ひさかたの
   　雨降らば降れ　風吹かば吹け
   Suteshi mi o　ikani to towaba　hisakata no
   　ame furaba fure　kaze fukaba fuke

3. Evening in the deep mountain
   All covered in white snow.
   I feel everything vanish,
   Yes, my soul and body, too.

   深山びの　雪ふりつもる　夕暮は
   　わが心さへ　消ぬべく思ほゆ
   Miyabi no　yuki furitsumoru　yūgure wa
   　waga kokoro sae　kenubeku omohoyu

4. Like a thread of water
   Trickling down the mossy rock,
   I'm growing clearer and clearer
   In the heart of the mountain.

   やまかげの　岩間をつたふ　苔水の
   　かすかにわれは　すみわたるかも
   Yamakage no　iwama o tsutau　kokemizu no
   　kasukani ware wa　sumiwataru kamo

5. Looking back these fifty years.
   Human good and evil seems
   Nothing but a dream in a dream,
   At midnight, I hear early summer rain
   Drizzling outside the solitary window.

半	山	人	回
夜	房	間	首
蕭	五	是	五
々	月	非	十
灑	黃	一	有
虛	梅	夢	余
窓	雨	中	年

6. Not even the shadow of a bird,
   Flying to the distant mountain,
   The falling leaves are frequent in the quiet yard,
   In the autumn wind
   A black-robed monk is standing alone.

獨	寂	閑	遠
立	莫	庭	山
緇	秋	落	飛
衣	風	葉	鳥
人	裡	頻	絕

7. Foolish and stubborn is my character,
   Can it be cured some day?
   I've been alone and poor all through my life,
   In the darkness, I'm walking back again,
   Along the lonely path from the village,
   Holding an empty bowl* in my hand.

   癡頑何日休
   孤貧是生涯
   日暮荒村路
   復揭空盂歸

8. All is silent
   But for the dead leaves falling.
   The essence of meditation lies in immobility.
   On it, I've concentrated my whole life,
   And yet,
   Why these tears?

   坐時聞落葉
   靜住是出家
   從來斷思量
   不覺淚沾巾

* a bowl used by monks for alms: usually called *hachi* or *hachinoko*

9. Rain goes, clouds go, the air is refreshed,
   My mind clears up, everything purified.
   Giving up this world, as well as myself,
   Changing into a useless being,
   Here am I,
   Spending the rest of my life,
   Enjoying the moon and the flowers to the full.

雨晴雲晴氣復晴
心清遍界物皆清
棄世棄身為閑者
初月與花送余生

Autumn Twilight

10. The autumn air is quiet and desolate
    Leaning against a staff, a monk stands in the chilly wind.
    A solitary village lies shrouded in the thick fog.
    A faint figure is seen on a bridge in the fields,
    Crows are returning to their nests in the old forests,
    Up in the darkling sky, a line of wild geese flying in the
         form—the last one fading into the darkness,
    Such is the scene, the black-robed monk stands still
    By the big river in the evening twilight.

秋氣何蕭索
倚杖稍寒裏
孤村風霧裏
行人苦橋邊
老鴉宿故林
斜雁沒遙天
唯有緇衣僧
立儘暮江前

Ryōkan's calligraphy.